"THE HIGHER CHRISTIAN LIFE"

SOURCES FOR THE STUDY OF THE HOLINESS, PENTECOSTAL, AND KESWICK MOVEMENTS

*A forty-eight-volume facsimile
series reprinting extremely
rare documents for the study of
nineteenth-century religious
and social history, the rise
of feminism, and the
history of the Pentecostal and
Charismatic movements*

Edited by

Donald W. Dayton
Northern Baptist Theological Seminary

Advisory Editors

D. William Faupel, *Asbury Theological Seminary*
Cecil M. Robeck, Jr., *Fuller Theological Seminary*
Gerald T. Sheppard, *Union Theological Seminary*

A GARLAND SERIES

FROM THE ALTAR TO THE UPPER ROOM

Ralph C. Horner

Garland Publishing, Inc.
New York & London
1984

For a complete list of the titles in this series
see the final pages of this volume.

Library of Congress Cataloging in Publication Data

Horner, Ralph C.
FROM THE ALTAR TO THE UPPER ROOM.

("The Higher Christian life")
Reprint. Originally published: Toronto :
W. Briggs, 1891.
1. Christian life.   I. Title.   II. Series.
BV4501.H5353 1984   230'.99   84-18847
ISBN 0-8240-6423-2 (alk. paper)

The volumes in this series are printed on
acid-free, 250-year-life paper.

Printed in the United States of America

FROM THE ALTAR

TO

THE UPPER ROOM

IN FOUR PARTS.

By REV. RALPH C. HORNER, B.O.

Author of " Voice Production," etc.

INTRODUCTION BY REV. A. CARMAN, D.D.

General Superintendent of the Methodist Church.

TORONTO:

WILLIAM BRIGGS,

WESLEY BUILDINGS.

C. W. COATES, Montreal, Que.   S. F. HUESTIS, Halifax, N.S.

WHILE regarding some of Bro. Horner's positions extreme, and some things laid on us in this first part from Christ's life that Christ Himself did not and does not lay upon us, owing to the differences of relation betwixt God and man, and man and man, I find many incisive, inspiring and instructive sentences, of great help to the soul in the honest work of spiritual self-examination. The danger of erring in practical Christian life is on the worldly and selfish side; hence strong representations of self-denial, self-humiliation, and constant looking to and trusting in that great sacrifice, the life and death of Christ, whose heights and depths we can never reach, but may alway seek, the better to show us how we should submit ourselves one to another in love, and in the fear of God. There is certainly no degradation in humbling ourselves in any act or effort to reconciliation after the mind of the adorable Lord. Bro. Horner presents this aspect of the Christian life very vigorously.

A. CARMAN.

PART I.

TO, BEFORE, AND ON THE ALTAR.

TO, BEFORE,

AND

ON THE ALTAR

BY

REV. RALPH C. HORNER, B.O.

Author of "Voice Production," Etc.

INTRODUCTION BY REV. A. M. PHILLIPS, B.D.

TORONTO:

WILLIAM BRIGGS,

WESLEY BUILDINGS.

MONTREAL: C. W. COATES.   HALIFAX: S. F. HUESTIS.

INTRODUCTION.

<hr/>

CHRISTIANITY is a spiritual religion adapted to the needs and circumstances of humanity. Its motive power is in the spirit, but its practical action is through the body. Its sphere of operation is pre-eminently in this world and for this life. Anything that contributes to the procuring of a true spirituality as the foundation of Christian character, and its application to every-day living ought to be hailed with delight. Such a contribution is here offered by Rev. Ralph C. Horner. His treatment of the subject will, no doubt, suggest heart-searching thought which, if applied to the individual life, must result in a truer Christianity.

The Christian religion, though divine in origin and power, is intensely human in application and result. Christ, in all His teaching, constantly enforced human relations. He was ever rebuking that hypocritical righteousness that centred in self, and constantly enforcing a sacrifice that was only surpassed by His own, that is, Christ made the very essence of His religious system to be a spirit of self-renunciation. He intended that the spirit that actuated His followers should be the same as that which controlled Himself. His great mission was securing the reconciliation of humanity to God. Therefore, in making reconciliation to man fundamental in order to a true reconciliation to God, He asks us simply to adopt His own principles of action. Bro. Horner's close application of Christ's method of cultivating the only right feeling toward our brother, is the one that is in harmony with the law of the life of God in relation to man. There can be no absolute reconciliation to God until in willingness of spirit and desire of heart (if not possible in fact), the soul seeking perfection is reconciled to any one whom he may remember has aught against him, as he waits the coming of the fire.

Bro. Horner is doubtless right in calling attention to the often overlooked fact that when we are in the right spirit ourselves, in the right relation to man, and in the right attitude to God, the baptism of fire is sure to come upon us. In other words, when we are emptied of self and our all is upon the altar, we will be filled with the Holy Spirit. The question, however, arises in our mind as to whether Christ is the altar of sanctification. Is he both priest to receive the gift, and altar to sanctify it? Is not humanity the real altar of consecration? Is there any consecration to God that is not a consecration to man? Is there any way of serving God but by serving our fellows? Is not the true idea, that we place ourselves at the disposal of our Heavenly Father, to be used by the Holy Spirit for the good of man and the glory of God, through Christ Jesus? The spirit and purpose of Bro. Horner is good, and the circulation of this pamphlet will be beneficial in leading others to a truer Christian life if they are thereby brought into a right feeling to their fellowmen. We would be pleased if we had more of this practical heart-searching teaching.

A. M. PHILLIPS.

TO, BEFORE, AND ON THE ALTAR.

BY REV. R. C. HORNER.

————

552 SHERBROOKE STREET,
MONTREAL, *May 7th, 1891.*

The reading of this short pamphlet will be of interest, and tend to the spiritual profit of many.

The truths it presents are of intrinsic value in the formation of Christian character, and their tendency will be to produce a more correct knowledge of the Christian's duty.

The duties of forgiveness, reconciliation and obedience are forcibly presented.

To some, the views presented will cause surprise, by more they will be rejected, by others explained away or toned down, but it will not be a task easy of accomplishment to destroy the claim of the author to Scriptural authority for his opinions.

His presentation of the necessity of obedience to the Divine command, rather than an evasion of it, or a supplanting of a Divine injunction by a self-selected and so-called sacrifice is well expressed in the following plain, pungent words, "There is nothing that will take the place of obedience to the Divine command. God hath said, 'First be reconciled to thy brother.' The Divine order must be observed. God did not give commands to be broken. To obey is better than to sacrifice."

A careful reading of this pamphlet, with a simple desire to rise to a clearer conception of duty, would be a great blessing to the individual Christian, and the faithful practice of its principles an untold benefit to the Church. It will well repay a careful reading.

T. G. WILLIAMS, D.D.,

President Montreal Conference.

CONTENTS.

TO, BEFORE, AND ON THE ALTAR.

I T is not a very difficult matter to get most professors of religion to come into a prayer circle for the purpose of consecrating themselves entirely to God. Many of them are honest and sincere. Every time an appeal is made, they seem to be anxious and ready to advance. Still they go through the whole procedure as a mere matter of form. Their faith is weak and their love is cold. When they are closely questioned regarding their spiritual attainments, they will affirm, with emphasis, that they have their all upon the altar. They will declare positively, that they have given their all to Christ, that they do not hold back anything from Him. They wonder why

they do not receive the blessing that they feel
they need.   They are just waiting for the fire to
come down and consume their sacrifice, and they
wonder why it does not come.   They are conscious that they are not saved from all sin.
They do not blame themselves for not having
received full salvation.   They believe that they
have done their part, and they are waiting for
the Lord to do His.   They say that they expect
to receive it in God's own good time, that when
He sees fit He will accept their offering, and
save them from all their sins.   They have not
yet learned that now is God's time, they are not
anxious about it, they are only waiting.   The
altar to them is a cold place, similar to the old
Jewish altars of brick, stone and mortar.   Their
only hope lies in the expected descent of
fire, to burn their offering and make them
every whit whole.   Many of them are sincere; they desire to be saved from all inbred
sin; they wish to be useful in the vineyard of
the Lord, but their conceptions of the altar are
very vague.   The altar with some of them is
only an imaginary thing; they have nothing to

rest on; they have no place to put their sacrifice, and they have no High Priest to accept their offering when they bring it.   Others bring their offerings and wish to present them, and they talk to the Lord about them.   They tell Him that they give their all to Him, but when they get off their knees, they carry everything away with them.   They carry around their burdens, and they groan under the weight, but will not cast them upon the Lord.   They have not received the truth as it is in Jesus, that the altar sanctifieth the gift.   They sing, and many of them ought to know better,—" My all is on the altar, I am waiting for the fire."   This would be in keeping with the Jewish dispensation.   Under the Gospel there is no waiting. Since the day of Pentecost there is no such experience.   There is no such teaching in the epistles.   It is not in the experience or teaching of the apostles under the dispensation of the Spirit.   " Men loved darkness rather than light, because their deeds were evil."   When the children of God have been sinning, they do not care to come to Christ, knowing that their deeds would be reproved. They will make some excuse.

TO THE ALTAR.

" If thou bring thy gift to the altar, and there rememberest that thy brother hath ought against thee." When you get on your knees at the altar, which is Christ the Sanctifier, many things are remembered that had been forgotten for years. Some things will be revived which you had wished never to think of again. " He will guide you into all truth." The Holy Ghost helps the memory. He illuminates, drives away the mists, and makes the mind active. He quickens the reproductive faculty. Facts, circumstances, transactions and grudges which had been forgotten for years, are brought up fresh and vivid to the mind. The Spirit will bring to your memory some brother or sister who has ought against you. It may be that it will be no pleasure to you to have it reproduced. You may be tempted at the same time, to think that it will do positive harm, to have the matter brought up again. If you are not willing to do right, to level up with your brethren and sisters in the Church, you will likely make an excuse. If you have been trying to cover up something for years, and after having spent much time in making a safe burial, you become conscious in a moment that a resurrection has taken place, the experience will be painful to you. Differences between you and your brother of fifty years' standing, will spring up in a moment, when you bring your gift to the altar. Nothing can be done at the altar, until you go and be reconciled to your brother. How many try to pray over these things, and try to believe that they are all right. Others suppose that because a certain period of time has elapsed, that the matter should be all right now. A wrong never wears away. Time never changes a wrong into a right. Prayers may be offered, but they alone cannot effect a reconciliation. Faith may be exercised, but it will profit nothing. The wrong or grudge may be subdued and concealed, until the gift is brought to the altar, then, in a moment, it will be fully exposed. God does not cover up evil; He never hides sin, and He never justifies His children in trying to hide their sins. He hath said: " He that covereth his sins shall not prosper." Jesus did not come to cover up our sins, but to wash them away from us. His name was called Jesus, because He should save His people from their sins. It may be that you have been trying for years to get your all upon the altar, and have not succeeded. You declare that you have no hard feelings against any living soul; you have set all wrongs right; you have straightened up all your accounts; you have paid one hundred cents on the dollar; you have been doing your duty toward God and man; you have taken up every cross; you have forgiven all your enemies, and you do not hold any hard feelings against those who have wronged you; you pray for all your enemies; you would like to see the worst enemy you ever had receive the blessing of God. Are you sure that you have done all this? You are positive. You do not see how it is possible for God to require any more of you. God does require that you should do more. When you go to the altar and there remember that your brother has ought against you, the first thing you must do is to go and be reconciled to him. It may be that you do not know any reason he could possibly have for entertaining ought against you. He may always have been the recipient of your kindness, sympathy and love. You want to know if you must seek to be reconciled to those you have never wronged either in word or deed, but have loved, esteemed and helped in many ways. You must go to those against whom you have never said an unkind word, regarding their persons, their lives, their business or their reputations. You must go to those who have ought against you, to those who have purposely slandered you, to those who have said all manner of evil against you, knowing it to be false; to those who have tried to injure your character, to the persons who have tried to injure you in your business, to the individual that swindled you out of so much, to the man who is by fraud wearing your coat on his back, and has left you poor, scarcely able to make ends meet. You must go to the person who has ought against

2

you, even he has swindled you out of thousands and left you nothing on which to live. You always believed that you should go to those *you* had wronged, and make the matter right. You have known that you must forgive everybody, if you would receive forgiveness yourself. You have not taken into your creed that you must go to those who have ought against you, even you have done them no harm. There is nothing on earth or in hell to-day, that so hinders the cause of God as the differences between God's children, which they refuse to settle. God's own people are capable of doing His cause more harm than all the devils in hell.

BEFORE THE ALTAR.

" Leave there thy gift before the altar, and go thy way; first be reconciled to thy brother." It may be that you will ask the question, Why does God require this? The answer is, He always places the burden upon the person who is able to bear it. If you have been good and have done nothing wrong, God has been continually blessing you, and you ought to be able

to undertake something practical for the Master.
You should be able and willing to help the
weak and erring brother. Those who have
been doing wrong, have not been blessed in
their wrong-doing, and are too weak to come to
you to be reconciled. It is human to expect
the offender to go first to the offended. It is
spiritual and divine, to make it compulsory for
the offended to go first to the offender and seek
for reconciliation. If you would be spiritual
you must move and act along spiritual lines.
If you are perfectly humble, it will be a joy and
delight to do that which will bring most glory
to God. If you are not perfectly humble, that
which will be most humiliating will be the very
best thing that you can undertake. It may
seem hard to you, but God will not fail you.
He lifts up those who humble themselves; He
will not send you hence without His presence,
if you will only follow Him. God expects you
to possess and exemplify the Spirit of Christ in
all things. "If any man have not the Spirit of
Christ, he is none of His." You are to have
the mind of Christ; you are to do as Christ did.

" I have given you an example, that ye should
do as I have done to you." Christ never gave
you any offence; He never wronged you; He
did you no evil; He has always loved you; He
manifested His love by dying for you. You
have sinned against His great love; you have
despised His mercy and rejected His salvation.
Christ did not sit down and say, I will remain
here, and if you come and ask for mercy I will
forgive you. He followed you day and night
for years; He invited you; He pleaded with
you; He constrained with the power of His
love; He stood and knocked at the door of
your heart, while the door was bolted and
barred against Him. How often you despised
Him! How often you have grieved His tender,
compassionate heart! In His love and mercy
He did not cast you off. He now asks you to
go to your brother who has ought against you
and seek for reconciliation; to do as He has
done to you; to manifest His love toward your
brother; to go in His name 'and rescue that
perishing brother; to do once what He did for
you so many hundreds of times; to magnify

His grace in you. If the command were go, and the arrow of the Almighty will humiliate your brother, you would start immediately. The thought of seeing him get down on his knees to ask your pardon would be so pleasing to you, that you would go to him in haste. If your brother would with much penitence confess to you that he had wronged you, and desired very much to be forgiven, how quickly you would go to him. If he would make a public acknowledgment, before all the congregation, of the wrong he had done to you, how it would please you to listen to his confession. If he would only tell to the Church that you had always been a perfect angel among men, that he had wronged you because you were so good, how your soul would gloat over it. If you were assured that it would be inserted in all the papers, and thus spread broadcast throughout the community, that you were perfectly innocent, and your character so defended and eulogized that the community would wish to canonize you as a saint for your acts of humility, you would go and seek with all your heart for reconciliation. You are not to seek your own, but your brother's happiness. You are not to look upon your own, but the things of others. "Be not overcome of evil, but overcome evil with good." You plead that he would not listen to you, that it would only aggravate him, and make the matter worse. There is no doubt that it would only provoke him to go to him to prove to him that he had done wrong, and that you were the embodiment of perfection. Even you were to go in the spirit of prayer to his home, and the discussion is opened with prayer, it will profit nothing, so long as your object is to prove to him that he is wrong. You may know that he is wrong. Your brethren in the Church may know that you are innocent and that he is guilty. They may all unite with you in trying to prove that he is wrong, and when you get through it will be worse than when you commenced. You may prove to him that you are perfectly innocent. All the brethren may vindicate all that you have done, and when that is done, the case is not settled, but the difference is made greater. You may try him in every court of the Church, and thereby impede the work of God for months, and no good will come out of it. You will only succeed in accomplishing one thing by all these efforts, and that is this, you will drive him farther away from God. This is not God's way of doing it, and you will not have His blessing on it.

There is only one way of settling differences between the children of God. Human inventions only aggravate the offender. He will become completely soured. The consciousness that you are trying to prove that he is wrong will get up the fight in him. He will at once make up his mind that he will fight it through. It would be much better to leave the matter as it stands, than to try to prove that he is wrong. He will become more obstinate; his soul will become desperate; he will not ask God to help him; he will be off his guard; he will not think of the tempter, and he will set himself to contend with you. You will lose your influence over him. The enemy will come in upon him as a flood, and reconciliation will quickly become impossible, even in God's own way. He will commence to look on the people of God as being against him; he will readily conclude that they have no sympathy for him, and he will lose faith in them. The people of the world will sympathize with him and assure him that he is right, and that his brethren in the Church have wronged him. He will absent himself from the means of grace. His relations will sympathize with him, and he will prevent them receiving any good. It will be impossible to reach him; his influence for evil will be a potent factor. You cannot get your gift upon the altar until you are reconciled with your brother. You may pray about it for weeks, months or years, and still you will make no advancement. You may secure the prayers of your brethren, and they may have and exercise much faith, but they will avail nothing. You may claim your interest in the prayers of the good and holy of all the ages, and they will not help you the least. God will not hear prayer for you until you obey Him. You may listen to many divines preach, and be delighted with their expositions of truth, and their flights of oratory, but your gift will remain as it was *Before* but not *On* the altar. There is nothing that will take the place of obedience to the command of God. God hath said, "First be reconciled to thy brother." The divine order must be observed. God did not give commands to be broken. To obey is better than to sacrifice. You can have no help from God, until you do as He has told you. Your High Priest, the Lord Jesus Christ, will not accept of your gift until you comply with the conditions. It is not possible for Him to do it. The council of the Trinity cannot be altered. His oath cannot be broken. The truth cannot be changed; His word does not pass away. All must be fulfilled, "Go thy way, first be reconciled." Your gift will remain before the altar until the reconciliation has been effected. Your soul cannot be sanctified. You can make no advancement. You cannot grow in grace. You cannot be useful in the vineyard of the Lord. You must of necessity backslide, if you do not perform your duty at once, to bring about a reconciliation. Your soul will become hungry, weak, sickly, and will die. There is no help for you until you obey—" Go thy way." God's way—" Be reconciled to thy brother." You are to go to Him in that spirit, the spirit of reconciliation. Having no other feeling; harboring nothing else; putting away from you every other tendency; cultivating the spirit of reconciliation; praying for it; at any cost; at at any loss; in any way. Your being animated with that kind of a spirit; your soul permeated with it; your mouth filled with it. When you go to your brother with that kind of a spirit your very presence will touch a vital and sympathetic chord in his heart; your very look will speak volumes and allay prejudice. Opposition will immediately give way. The powers of darkness lose their force and power under such circumstances. The way will at once be opened up; you can assure him that you are reconciled to him. He cannot but feel it; his spirit will be at once humiliated; he will at once be overcome. He will unconsciously get under the power of the Spirit. He did not expect that kind of an interview, he will be thrown off his base, he will feel at once that he would like to undertake something humiliating. Then submit the case fully to himself for settlement; in his own way; at his own terms. Do not dictate to him; do not offer to help him; make no suggestions whatever; assure him that whatever he may do is already accepted by you freely. Press it upon him; assure him that he can settle the matter himself. He will probably suggest something. Perhaps he will leave it to the brethren. He will very likely confess to you that he has become sorry for saying and doing what he did; he will acknowledge that he did it without thinking; that he yielded to temptation. He will be relieved in mind and soul; his heart will warm toward you; he will accept you as one of his best friends; he will at once become humbled before God; his soul will be blessed; he will be completely restored; he will return to his post of duty. You will have saved him from going to the pit. The effect of the reconciliation among your brethren will be gracious. Sinners will be moved by it; the cause of God will revive in your midst; your

own soul will be strengthened and encouraged
by it; the smile of God will rest upon you.
Having become reconciled to your brother and
saved him, you can return to the altar and offer
your gift.

ON THE ALTAR.

"Then come and offer thy gift." The Lord
Jesus your High Priest will accept of your gift,
and will immediately place it upon the altar.
There will be accomplished in a moment what
you have been trying to realize for years. The
trying will all be over; you will not have to try
to be consecrated any more; you will be consecrated; you will know at once that you are consecrated; you will know that you kept nothing
in reserve. There will be a consciousness that
Jesus has accepted all; you will not be wishing
and hoping that it is so, you will know that it is
done. There will be no wish for something
great to take place. You will have no time to
wish, to hope, or to surmise. The Lord Jesus
Himself being the altar, there will be no waiting
for fire; there will be no pleading for fire to come

down and consume the sacrifice. You will not
have to try to feel the fire burning, and you will
have no time to think whether you feel as
others have described it or not. Having had
faith enough in Jesus to trust Him with your
gift by giving it into His possession, He lets the
refining fire go through you. The altar sanctifies
the gift. The fire does not come streaming
down from heaven, it goes up from the altar and
purifies everything within reach of it. The fire
melts, moulds, and refines all that is placed upon
the altar. The very moment that the Lord
Jesus receives the offering it is sanctified wholly.
The whole nature is purged and purified from
all the defilement of the flesh and spirit. It is
made free from indwelling sin. Every evil tendency is destroyed, every evil propensity is
completely removed. Anger, wrath, malice,
envy, selfishness, fear, pride, etc., are entirely
separated from the soul. The soul is at once
filled with love, joy, peace, etc. The soul will
know no fear, perfect love having cast it all out.
Trouble completely ceases. When all has been
given to Christ there is nothing to be troubled

about. The soul will be dead to sin and alive to
God. The faith will cling to all the promises of
God. Trusting will be as natural as breathing.
The joy of the Lord will be the strength of the
soul. Love for God and man will have become
perfect. The soul will never be satisfied only
when it is achieving glorious victories for Jesus.
The special anointing of the Spirit for service
will be received as soon as it is known to be the
privilege of the sanctified soul.

PART II.

WHAT IS CONSECRATION?

WHAT IS CONSECRATION?

BY

REV. RALPH C. HORNER, B.O.

Author of " Voice Production," Etc

TORONTO:

WILLIAM BRIGGS,

WESLEY BUILDINGS.

C. W. COATES, Montreal,   S. F. HUESTIS, Halifax.

WHAT IS CONSECRATION ?

1. It is a just and reasonable demand of God, since He is our Creator, Father, Preserver, Redeemer, Friend, He has a right to claim our affection and service.

2. It is to turn from all ungodliness and worldly lusts, to come out from the world, to be separate, to touch not the unclean thing, to shun the way of evil-doers, to seek peace and ensue it.

3. It is humble submission to the claims and injunctions of the Word of God, to accept the law as our schoolmaster to bring us to Christ; not to question, but to yield fully, and obey perfectly all the commands.

4. It is the deliberate choice of Christ as our Saviour, with the sneer of the ungodly, the

malice of the devil, the protest of hell, the frown of the world, the contempt of formalists ; for the privilege of communion with Him, to share a part in His kingdom, and a seat on His throne.

5. It is to be humble, devoted, agreeable, and exemplify a Christ-like spirit, to live soberly, righteously and godly in this present evil world·

6. It is a solemn and complete dedication of ourselves, our friends, our goods, our honors, our affections, and all that we highly esteem on earth, to our Lord and Saviour Jesus Christ.

7. It is to resist the devil with vigilance and sobriety, to confide in the promises of God as the only possible way of becoming a partaker of the Divine nature.

8. It is to be God's child, to love Him, to obey Him in all things, to give testimony to His saving power, to bear every cross, to do every duty, and to walk well-pleasing in His sight.

9. It is to be dead indeed unto sin, and alive unto God, to count all things loss for the excellency of the knowledge of Christ, to have the full assurance of faith, hope and understanding,

to be begotten, sanctified, and kept a vessel unto honor meet for the Master's use.

10. It is to have no fellowship with the unfruitful works of darkness, but to reprove them by a well-ordered life and a godly conversation, to have communion with God and His people.

11. It is the entire surrender of body, soul, spirit, time, talents, influence, reputation, memory, mind, will, possessions, acquirements, expectations, honors, all that we have, all that we ever hoped for, to be the property of the Lord.

12. It is to consider that our best thought, our warmest energy, our purest affections, our noblest consecration of purpose, our most solemn devotion, our capabilities and possibilities, are His by redemption.

13. It is to be able to express from the heart : I am not my own, I have nothing, I desire nothing, I am crucified with Christ, I am dead to sin, I am alive to God, I am a broken and emptied vessel, I am weaker than a bruised reed, and Christ is all and in all.

14. It is to place a bridle on the tongue, to bind the unruly member to the altar, to preserve the law of truth, to allow no corrupt communication to proceed out of the mouth, to use sound speech which cannot be condemned, to have all our words and expressions seasoned with grace.

15. It is to be conscious that my body is the temple of the Holy Ghost, my soul is His habitation, my intellect is His to be developed for Him, my affections are centered upon Him, my will delights in His law, my time is being spent as He dictates, my talents are being used only for His glory, my silver and gold are for the advancement of His cause, and all my faculties of mind and soul are being used in His service.

16. It is life, time, talents, intellect, means, affections, capability of usefulness, natural gifts and privileges bestowed upon me by my Father, utilized for the extension of His kingdom, the promotion of His work, and the glory of His name.

17. It is to have all on the altar, to know that the altar is not cold, to feel that it is red

hot, to be purified as silver, to be refined as gold by the fire.

18. It is to live a pure, holy, devoted, blameless life, to be a burning and shining light, to spread scriptural holiness throughout the land, and adorn this blessed doctrine of God our Saviour.

19. It is loyalty to God, to His cause, to His people, in heart and life, in all manner of conversation, at any cost, sacrifice, loss or peril, for all time, through evil as well as good report, in sickness and in health.

20. It is self-denial of food that would injure the system, of clothing that does not become persons professing godliness, as gold, feathers, etc., of pleasure that has the appearance of evil, of everything that does not glorify God.

21. It is that fulness of God's love in the soul which makes duty a pleasure, suffering for God's cause and glory a delight, temptation and persecution a source of blessing, the battles we have to fight our joy, being able to shout victory before we enter the contest.

22. It is to be hated of all men for Christ's sake, to be singular among men, to be fools for the sake of Jesus, to be godly and thereby suffer persecution for the Redeemer's sake.

23. It is to "take pleasure in infirmities, in reproaches, in necessities, in persecutions, in distresses for Christ's sake," to count it all joy, to sink deeper and rise higher.

24. It is to rejoice and be exceeding glad in fiery trials, if we are thereby made partakers of Christ's sufferings, and glory in tribulations, counting not our lives dear, that we may run our course with the divine approval.

25. It is divinely begotten and inspired heroism, which endures all things for Christ's sake, stands every storm, faces every foe, vanquishes all opposition, puts to flight the armies of the aliens, dares to be peculiar for God, will dare to do His will, and would die rather than not do it, and can do all things through Christ.

26. It is pressing on incessantly toward the mark for the prize, forgetting the things which are behind, running the race with patience, looking unto Jesus, the author, until He becomes the finisher of our faith.

27. It is to set the affections on things above, and have a treasure in heaven, to mortify and overcome, to keep our bodies under, to put off anger, wrath, malice, envy, etc. ; to put on bowels of mercies, kindness, humbleness of mind, meekness, long-suffering, to put on charity, which is the bond of perfectness.

28. It is to endure hardness as good soldiers of Jesus Christ, to consider Him who endured, lest we be weary and faint in our minds ; to have the mind which was also in Christ.

29. It is to do all things in the name of the Lord Jesus, to go where He would have us go, to do what He would have us do, to seek the blessing of God on all we undertake, and whether we eat or drink, do all to the glory of God.

30. It is to walk worthy of God in all lowliness and meekness, to be diligent in all we undertake, to be fervent and spiritual in all acts of worship, and watching thereunto with all long-suffering and godliness.

31. It is to follow peace with all men, to know that in every case it takes two to make a fight ;

to live holy lives, to get holiness before we attempt to live it; to have that holiness without which no man can see the Lord, to show ourselves approved.

32. It is to be workmen that needeth not to be ashamed; to rightly divide the word of truth; to teach, admonish, exhort, entreat and rebuke with all authority; to be true to the doctrines of salvation, to lead others into Beulah land.

33. It is to be true to our leader on the battle-field, to have on the whole armor, to be in the front of the battle, to fight the good fight of faith, to be more than conquerors through Him who hath loved us, saved and washed us in His own most precious blood.

34. It is to be everything that it is possible for us to be for the Lord—this we owe to ourselves and to God; to be fully the Lord's, to be the best the Lord can make out of the material that is in us, to be developed according to our capability.

35. It is to regard life as a sum of money to be spent for God, in His own way, place, sphere; to wish for nothing, to will only His own will,

to be led in His way, which is known only to Himself.

36. It is to feel that sinners must not go to hell, to have faith for their present salvation, to know that God will answer our prayers for them; to not be able to rest or sleep until we see God's cause reviving, and sinners coming to Christ for salvation.

37. It is to have abiding fellowship with God, and such harmony with the operations of the Holy Ghost, that He can inspire our petitions, and increase our faith's capacity for the salvation of souls, so that it will be so hard for sinners to go to hell, that they will choose to turn and accept Christ.

38. It is to know that there are prevalent evils which we can prevent, to feel that God has filled our hearts with His love for a purpose, to be deeply impressed that God will use our honest efforts, and many can be turned from sin to love and serve God.

39. It is to be conscious of strength to bear the infirmities of our weak brethren, to be in perfect sympathy with those who are led

astray, to prevent the sweeping desolations of intemperance by voting, praying, talking and working against it.

40. It is to prevent Sabbath desecration, by inducing the masses to attend a place of worship; to instruct the ignorant and fallen in the way of life, to be leading some soul to Christ every day, to attend to all the means of grace, to rescue the perishing, to care for the dying, to lead many to Christ.

" To do or not to do, to have
    Or not to have, I leave with Thee;
To be or not to be, I leave;
    Thy only will be done in me;
All my requests are lost in one,
Father, Thy only will be done.

" Welcome alike the cross, the crown;
    Trouble I cannot ask, nor peace,—
Nor toil, nor rest, nor gain, nor loss,
    Nor joy, nor grief, nor pain, nor ease,
Nor life, nor death,—but ever groan,
Father, Thy only will be done."

PART III.

ENTIRE CONSECRATION.

ENTIRE CONSECRATION.

BY

REV. RALPH C. HORNER, B.O.

Author of "Voice Production," Etc.

INTRODUCTION

BY REV. A. CARMAN, D.D.

General Superintendent of the Methodist Church.

TORONTO

WILLIAM BRIGGS,

WESLEY BUILDINGS.

Montreal: C. W. COATES.   Halifax: S. F. HUESTIS.

INTRODUCTION.

WHILE not fathoming, endorsing, or attempting to explain the metaphysical or theological parts of Bro. Horner's little book on ENTIRE CONSECRA-TION, I cheerfully say I am very favorably impressed with the practical portions of the work, and think that his suggestive and natural divisions, earnest sentences, plain and direct statements, and cogent enforcement of Scriptural quotations, will, with all professing Christians—especially hesitating professors, languid souls—do much good. " But you will not get languid souls to start reading such a book." I think myself they would have read more eagerly and vigorously, taken more kindly to the bracing air, if the practical part of the work had been first in order; for there is something very taking to people that have any spiritual experience at all in Bro. Horner's terse and crisp utterances on this most important theme. Entire consecration, with what precedes, attends and follows it, is the great present want of the Church, and there can be no better point of view over the whole scene than a faithful treatise on this glorious subject.   He helps us much who helps us to consecration to God.   Bro. Horner writes like a living man, and will lead others to life and light.   God bless him and his book.

A. CARMAN.

CONTENTS.

ENTIRE CONSECRATION.

THERE are four distinct and separate parts in consecration. Through these varied experiences the soul must pass before it is entirely sanctified. Two of them are negative in their character and two positive. *First*, Submission to the divine will unto repentance and faith; *Second*, Dedication of the new-born soul to the service of God; *Third*, Entire submission unto repentance of inbred sin; *Fourth*, Entire consecration of every member of body, of every faculty of mind and soul, when purified by the sanctifying power of the Holy Ghost, to be filled and kept full of the love of God, and used in joyful service for God's glory.

SUBMISSION.

The surrender of the will to the Spirit's unfolding, of the teachings of the law, to the mind and conscience, is a necessary precursor of repentance toward God, and faith in the Lord Jesus Christ. In every case consecration in this form must precede repentance. Repentance is the gift of God, through the mediation of Jesus Christ, to the humiliated soul who submits to the will of the Father, as indicated by the operation of the Holy Ghost on the mind and conscience of the sinner.

In this way the negative side of consecration merges into and coincides with repentance and faith. Just as faith is consequent upon repentance, so repentance is dependent upon submission. Genuine repentance is the natural result of a thorough submission and sinking into the will of God, as faith in Jesus Christ is the natural successor of a godly sorrow for sin; or theologically, they are the gift of God to the soul that has yielded to the operation of the Spirit. Genuine conversion to God is almost wholly dependent upon the nature and extent of negative consecration, repentance and faith being preceded by it and made possible by its thoroughness, or so hindered that the soul

remains in darkness and is finally lost. An
incident is related of a missionary and a proud
and powerful Indian chief. The chief was convinced of sin. Trembling under a sense of guilt,
he approached the missionary and proffered his
belt of wampum to be freed from his crushing
fears. "No," said the missionary, "Christ
cannot accept such a sacrifice." The Indian
departed, but soon returned, offering his wife
and the skins he had taken in hunting. "No,"
was the reply, "Christ cannot accept such a
sacrifice." Again the Indian went away, but
soon returned once more with a troubled conscience, and offered his wigwam, wife, child,
everything, for pardon. "No," was still the
reply, "Christ cannot accept such a sacrifice."
The chief seemed oppressed for a moment, then,
lifting up tearful eyes to the face of the missionary, he feelingly cried out: "Here, Lord,
take poor Indian, too."

CONSECRATION.

Sonship is retained by the positive side of
consecration being fully developed by perfect
obedience. Every member of the body, every

capacity of the mind, and every faculty of the soul having been consecrated to God in a passive sense in order to attain unto repentance and saving faith. This saving relation is retained by an active consecration of all the natural gifts to the service of God. Every cross is taken up. Active consecration bears all the crosses. Some crosses are not heavy, and it is a pleasure to bear them. Those which are heavy and hard to bear are not despised, but are borne cheerfully. Every command claims perfect obedience. It is a pleasure to the regenerated soul to obey many commands. Consecration means that those commands which seem to be hard, dark and mysterious are cheerfully obeyed according to the strict letter of the law. Every duty toward God and man is discharged. Duty at times is a pleasure to the true child of God, but consecration makes it equally binding when it is painful, and sustains such a relation between the soul and God that there is no lack of power to do the will of God in all things. The active, consecrated soul does not object to work because it is unpleasant, and will undertake with enthusiasm that which is humiliating, painful and laborious. Consecration ceases to be complete when nothing is undertaken which causes the soul to agonize before God for help. Knowledge, wisdom and power are to be sought, in order that the whole duty may be done in such a manner as to bring the most possible glory to God.

Consecration places every member of the body under the direct operation of the Holy Ghost, every faculty of the soul at the disposal of the Spirit for joyful service, every capacity of the mind at God's disposal for intelligent service, and every organ of speech to be controlled and used only for God's glory.

The following words were the expression of President Jonathan Edwards when consecrating himself to God's service: "I have been before God, and have given myself, all that I am and have, to God, so that I am not in any respect my own; I can challenge no right in myself; I can challenge no right in this understanding, this will, these affections that are in me; neither have I any right to this body nor any of its members; no right to this tongue, these hands, nor feet ; no right to these senses, these eyes, these ears, this smell or taste. I have given myself clear away, and have not retained anything as my own. I have been to God this morning, and told Him that I give myself wholly to Him. I have given every power to Him, so that for the future I will challenge no right in myself in any respect. I have expressly promised Him, and do now promise Almighty God, that by His grace I will not. I have this morning told Him that I did take Him for my whole portion and felicity, looking on nothing else as any part of my happiness, nor acting as if it were ; and His law for the constant rule of my obedience ; and would fight with all my might against the world, the flesh, and the devil, to the end of my life ; that I did believe in Jesus Christ, and receive Him as a prince and a Saviour, and would adhere to the faith and obedience of the Gospel, how hazardous and difficult soever the profession and practice of it may be ; that I did receive the blessed Spirit as my teacher, sanctifier and only comforter, and cherish all His motions to enlighten, purify, confirm, comfort and assist me. This I have done. And I pray God, for the sake of Christ, to look upon it as a self-dedication, and to receive me as entirely His own, and deal with me in all respects as such, whether He afflicts me, or whatever He pleases to do with me, who am His. Now, henceforth I am not to act in any respect as my own. I shall act as my own if I ever make use of any of my powers to do anything that is not to the glory of God, and do not make the glorifying Him my whole and entire business; if I murmur in the least at afflictions; if I grieve at the prosperity of others; if I am in any way uncharitable; if I am angry because of injuries; if I revenge; if I do anything purely to please myself, or if I avoid anything for the sake of ease; if I omit anything because it is great self-denial; if I trust to myself; if I take any of the praise of any good that I do, or rather, which God does by me; or if I am any way proud." Observe how minute, particular, and complete is the consecration of this man of God.

" Dear Lord, only Thee !
    Only Thee, I pray ;
Fill my heart with only Thee
    Till I pass away.
Many do I love,
    And many do love me ;
But Thou—Thou all above—
    ' Thou knowest I love Thee ! ' '

" Dear Lord, be Thou my guide ;
    I give my hand to Thee !
By day and night, through time and tide,
    I know Thou wilt keep me.
The fairest love is mine
    Which in this world may be ;
Dear Lord, let ever mine be Thine ;
    ' Thou knowest I love Thee !' "

ENTIRE SUBMISSION.

As the negative side of consecration precedes
repentence and faith leading to justification ; so
it is also the forerunner of that repentance and
faith which is essential and leads to entire
sanctification.   Entire sanctification being a
deeper work than that experienced in the soul
at regeneration, and having more direct bearing
upon Christian work and usefulness, it is
obvious that consecration is almost entirely con-

fined to that part of Christian experience. The unregenerated soul is incapable of making a complete consecration. It must necessarily be imperfect on account of the weakness, darkness, and ignorance of the depraved heart. When the soul is regenerated, the Holy Spirit gives power to the believing heart, and every faculty can be more fully dedicated to the worship and service of God. The change is from darkness into light; the clear light of the Gospel dispelling the darkness, makes it possible to make a more thorough consecration of the redeemed powers to God. The regenerated soul, through the operation of the Spirit, receives a knowledge of divine things and a capability for intelligently dedicating every faculty to its particular function. The conviction of sin which precedes entire sanctification, being deeper than that experienced before justification, the light will thereby be increased and the possibilities of the human soul made much clearer. The spirit of consecration will consequently be deeper and broader, entering more fully into the hidden depths of the soul. Consecration must enter

every avenue, every faculty, every power of the
soul, into all the resources, if the work of repentance and faith is thorough and genuine, so that
the whole nature will be entirely sanctified and
enjoy all the fulness, clearness and completeness
of the blessing.   Entire consecration in this
form must precede entire sanctification, it is its
natural precursor.   Consecration in the form of
entire submission is very clearly and fully set
forth in one of Wesley's " Forms of Prayer," as
follows :

"To Thee, O God, Father, Son and Holy
Ghost, my Creator, Redeemer and Sanctifier, I
give up myself entirely ; may I no longer serve
myself, but Thee, all the days of my life.

" I give Thee my understanding ; may it be
my only care to know Thee, Thy perfections,
Thy works, and Thy will.   Let all things else
be as dung and dross unto me for the excellency
of this knowledge.   And let me silence all
reasonings against whatsoever Thou teachest
me, who canst neither deceive nor be deceived.

" I give Thee my will ; may I have no will of
my own ; whatsoever Thou willest may I will,

and that only. May I will Thy glory in all things, as Thou dost, and make that my end in every thing; may I ever say with the Psalmist, ' Whom have I in heaven but Thee ? and there is none upon earth that I desire beside Thee.' May I delight to do Thy will, O God, and rejoice to suffer it; whatever threatens me, let me say, 'It is the Lord, let Him do what seemeth Him good;' and whatever befalls me, let me give thanks, since it is thy will concerning me.

" I give Thee my affections; do Thou dispose of them all; be Thou my love, my fear, my joy; and may nothing have any share in them, but with respect to Thee and for Thy sake. What Thou lovest, may I love; what thou hatest, may I hate; and that in such measure as Thou art pleased to prescribe me.

" I give Thee my body; may I glorify Thee with it and preserve it holy, fit for Thee, O God, to dwell in. May I neither indulge it, nor use too much rigor towards it; but keep it, as far as in me lies, healthy, vigorous and active, and fit to do Thee all manner of service which Thou shalt call for.

2

" I give Thee all my worldly goods; may I prize them and use them only for Thee; may I faithfully restore to Thee, in the poor, all Thou hast entrusted me with, above the necessaries of life; and be content to part with them, too, whenever Thou, my Lord, shalt require them at my hands.

" I give Thee my credit and reputation; may I never value it, but only in respect of Thee; nor endeavor to maintain it, but it may do Thee service and advance Thy honor in the world.

" I give Thee myself and my all; let me look upon myself to be nothing, and to have nothing out of Thee. Be Thou the sole disposer and governor of myself and my all; be Thou my portion and my all." What a comprehensive consecration! How clear and concise, the blood-bought privilege of all the children of God.

ENTIRE CONSECRATION.

Consecration is entire when every member of the body, every faculty of the mind and soul are purified from sin, filled with the love of God, and dedicated to His service. This consecration, connected with all that has preceded it, is holiness. Consecration had to be entire in a negative sense, reaching forward and attaining unto entire sanctification. This experience is retained by a positive consecration of the fulness of love to God in active service, as dictated by the Word of God and the Holy Ghost. That which is reserved and not dedicated to God cannot be set apart, purified, energized, and used by the Holy Ghost.

Entire sanctification is not only purification from sin, but the full consecration of love to Christ—then it is holiness. When the Holy Spirit is purifying the nature He does not store away any member of the body, any power of the mind, any faculty of the soul, but seals them for divine service ; and entire consecration is that energy of the soul by which every part performs its function. The consecration which follows entire sanctification must, of necessity, be deeper and broader than that which preceded it. The consecration which succeeds regeneration and precedes entire sanctification may be and is generally carried into effect, and incited by duty; but that which follows entire sanctification is propelled by love. Love having become supreme in all things. The cross having become a privilege, and duty a joy and delight. The soul filled with love to God delights to obey Him. Then neighbors and enemies are loved, and the soul yearns for their salvation. Praying and trusting are like breathing, they have become perfectly natural, and are vigorously prosecuted without any conscious effort. "The Spirit is imparted in His fulness for the entire consecration of the soul to the triune God; the love of God having its perfect work in us, is the instrument of our deliverance from indwelling sin; and the return of our love made perfect also is the strength of our obedience unto entire holiness." Divine love is the principle of consecration, awakening our love, as the principle of personal dedication. The Word of God is the instrument which the Holy Ghost uses in effecting entire sanctification—He sanctifies through the truth, not apart from it.

MORTIFICATION.

To mortify is to kill. Mortification means death. Physicians dread it. Human nature succumbs to its destroying properties when an antidote is not speedily administered. Mortification is an indispensable accompaniment of consecration in its various forms. It is mortification that makes consecration difficult. Self dies hard. Every propensity of the rebellious nature refuses to die and struggles to live. When habit has become permanently seated, and is indulged regularly in the routine of life, it is thereby a part of self, and dies very reluctantly. Any selfish, slothful or filthy habit indulged in, will, through course of time, become so fully a part of the being that human nature will claim that it has a right to exist. The Saviour understood this when He said, " If the right eye offend thee, pluck it out." To speak of the habits of some of God's children is like gouging the eye out of the head, and the eye must come out. " If thy right hand offend thee, cut it off, and cast it from thee." When physicians have said

that it was the only means, the last remedy at
their disposal to save the life; the afflicted have
chosen death rather than part with the right
hand. Those who submit to the operation and
part with a member, do it very reluctantly. In
like manner some give up the service of Christ,
with all their prospects of a future state of happiness, rather than deny themselves of certain
filthy, unholy, degrading habits. A clear, close,
full application of God's law would drive away
the multitude, and the number will be reduced,
as it was under the Saviour's preaching to the
eleven. And the question may be asked, will
you also go away? Since God has promised to
cleanse away all filthiness of the flesh, and all
our idols, we are without excuse, and should
claim the privilege and rejoice therein. "Then
will I sprinkle clean water upon you, and ye
shall be clean: from all your filthiness, and from
all your idols, will I cleanse you." He has
promised to make our bodies the temple of the
Holy Ghost, that He will dwell and walk in us.
"Ye are the temple of the living God; as God
hath said, I will dwell in them, and walk in

them; I will be their God, and they shall be My people." The promise is conditional, and is not fulfilled until God's requirements are met. The members are to be mortified and overcome, in order to escape the wrath of God which cometh upon the children of disobedience. "Mortify therefore your members." We are called to be honorable vessels, "sanctified and meet for the Master's use," and "thoroughly furnished unto all good works." The youthful lusts must be arrested, mortified and overcome, and repented of at the feet of Jesus, where the cleansing efficacy of the (Saviour's) blood will thoroughly purge away all tendencies and propensities of inbred sin, it will completely erase the original offence. The blood does not cleanse until sin is mortified and repented of, by a far deeper conviction than that experienced before regeneration. We are debtors to ourselves and to God, not to live after the flesh, but by the power of the Spirit to mortify the deeds of the body and live. The body being the temple of the Holy Ghost, it is not of ourselves, nor for ourselves, but we have it of God; and we are not our own, for we are bought with a price. They are to be purified, sanctified, nourished, cherished, preserved and kept for the Master's use. The old man having been put off, his deeds also which are deceitful according to the depraved lusts are to be put away without any reserve. The conversation is to be in heaven, and foolish talking and jesting which are not convenient are not to be indulged in or encouraged. Those who continue to be Christ's crucify the flesh with the affections and lusts, and are not desirous of vainglory, but they provoke one another to love and good works. They do not serve, but they destroy the body of sin, neither do they yield their members as servants of sin; but dedicate themselves to God, they have their fruit unto holiness and the end everlasting life. Building up themselves for a habitation of God, who has put His law into their inward parts, and hath written it on their hearts.

OBJECT.

The purpose in consecration must not be merely to be happy, to have good feelings, a pleasant time, the joy that others speak of; that would be in the fullest sense selfishness. It is not feeling we are to seek, but Christ the Saviour; not pleasure, but the will of the Master; not a happy frame of mind, but the cleansing virtue of the Saviour's blood. What God requires is not gifts, services, sacrifices, but our own selves, to surrender our free conscious selves to Christ, to absolutely give up our own wills, and to accept the will of the Christ for the government of our lives. The highest possible motive must prompt the souls of those who seek for full conformity to the divine will, and the fulness of the blessing of the Gospel of Christ. The soul presented to God in consecration must be placed on the altar of sacrifice to suffer the righteous will of a loving Father, who will give joy or sorrow, health or sickness, life or death, ease or hardship, pleasure or pain, peace or trouble, as seemeth good to Him, for His own glory, and the eternal blessedness of His child. "He himself must bring the sacrifice and lay it upon the altar." God will have a voluntary service or none. This may be a

difficult work. It always is. The will bends
reluctantly; self pleads persuasively; unbelief
suggests a thousand fears: the great adversary,
and all the influences which operate upon the
soul in opposition to God, combine to prevent
such a step. But it can be taken, and it must
be taken. The will must yield, self must be
denied, only God must be trusted, the devil
resisted, and the offering made." It may not,
and will not be all smooth sailing when the
consecration is complete. God's ways are ways
of pleasantness, yet, He scourgeth every son
whom He receiveth. "No chastening for the
present seemeth to be joyous, but grievous,
nevertheless afterward it yieldeth the peaceable
fruit of righteousness unto them which are
exercised thereby." Temptations, persecutions,
and trials will be numerous. The closer we live
to God, and the more fully we are endued with
power from on high, the greater efforts the
world and the devil will make to discourage us
in our work of faith and labor of love. The
soul which settles down into a passive state
has been captivated and possessed by a most

dangerous delusion. Consecration must be active, as well as passive, to accomplish the will of God, to bear the solemn protest of hell, to quench the fiery darts of the devil, to ward off the chilling winds of formalism, and to endure the cruel contempt of an ungodly world. Consecration must be made for the glory of God, at any cost or loss, at any exposure, for any purpose, in the face of death. A joyful dedication of all the ransomed powers, and specifically carried out in the minutest details. This consecration is not made with reluctance, but deliberately and with enthusiasm. The whole soul is so enamored with the cause of Christ and his redemptive glory, that hardship and loss is esteemed a pleasure. The will of God in everything is supreme, and every uprising in the unsanctified heart is crucified. The opposition is great and potent. The stubborn will does not submit readily. It makes its last mighty struggle before it yields fully and submits to everything. The pride of the human heart refuses to be humbled in this last great struggle for existence. The fears assail with threatening, the road appears rough, moles are magnified into mountains. But in spite of pride, in spite of fear, in spite of the devil, all is laid on the altar for active service. The claim of God upon His children is entire conformity to His will, and whether it is pleasant or painful it is undertaken and perpetuated. The heavy cross is accompanied with the greatest blessing. Vigorous exercise develops strong muscle; and it is the severe test that develops faith most rapidly. "That the trial of your faith, being much more precious than of gold that perisheth, though it be tried with fire, might be found unto praise, and honor, and glory at the appearing of Jesus Christ."

CONSECRATED ELOQUENCE.

It may be that you are one of those who try to apologize for your sin by saying that you have no talent. It is wicked for you not to use the gift that God has given you; but it is atrocious to lie in order to justify yourself before men, by declaring that God did not give you the gift of speech for speaking and praying.

The Saviour discussed this important question, as He did all truth essential to the plan of salvation. He said that some have five talents, some have two, and others have one, but none have less than one, yet you say that He did not give you a talent for speaking. Any candid person would be ready to admit that if you could not converse about other things, that you could not talk for Jesus; but can you not entertain your friends in conversation concerning other subjects which are of very little importance ? A very large majority of people can talk fluently about what concerns them most. He who has set his heart on money finds no difficulty in expressing himself on that important subject. He can talk when he trades. He can uphold his side of a bargain with precision and power. He makes the money come when he speaks. There is no eloquence or oratory that can persuade him to part with it. When he has gained possession his hold is firm, and the force and readiness with which he talks about his possessions are truly amazing. The more he gets the more eloquent he becomes, so that he can talk about it fluently. His consecration to money-making has assumed a perfect form, and his soul has become fired with its inspiring energy, so that the love of it has become to him the root of all evil. Money has become his god; the more he possesses, and the longer he worships it, the more humbly he bows and devotes himself to his idol. The worldling who is getting hold of all the land he can secure, and whose buildings must be after a certain fashion, and everything according to his ambition, will toil and tug until his back has become crooked, his whole being out of shape, and his constitution completely shattered. He is thoroughly consecrated. He has a purpose. He has one special object in life, and he is devoted to it. Can he talk about his god? Go to see him in his home, but don't go when he is crowded with work, or he would not take time to look at you. Call to see him after he has had a heavy siege of toil, when nothing in particular is pressing him or appealing to his ambitious soul. He will escort you to every field on his farm, and describe in the minutest detail the quality of the soil, and how he prepared it for the seed. He can tell you the name and the quality of the seed sown, and weigh out to you in the balance of his mind how much he expects off the acre. He can express the good qualities of every horse with an artistic finish of diction; and language, rhetoric or fluency do not fail, but increase in quality and quantity, as his soul gloats over the work of hands. His florid utterances when describing his cattle, sheep, etc., are embellished with a finish of eloquence which is the spontaneous outburst of a soul fully consecrated to the object of his choice. His tongue seems to have been endowed with a sort of perpetual motion. The longer he talks about them the more fluent he becomes. Why? His heart is bound up in them. It seems to be as easy for him to talk as to breathe. Ask him to lead in prayer before you part with him, and he will declare positively that God gave him no talent.

When a chair has been vacated in the House of Assembly, and the people are called upon to elect their representative, immediately every mind is charged, every heart is full, every

mouth is open and every tongue is loosened.
The papers are read and information is gathered
from every source. All who take the rostrum
have a hearing. Not a single complaint is heard
with reference to the inability of any one to
express himself. Almost every person has
become eloquent. There seems to be no lack
of practical oratory. Orators are born of the
occasion. Most men you meet can give you
their politics and your own. None are willing
to take a back seat. All press for the front.
Every person almost expects a hearing. All
feel confident that they are right. They are
unwilling to flinch for their superiors. Men
will hail you on the street, and pour a stream of
red-hot politics upon you, and catch the flame
you must. Nearly every man you meet is ready
to take the stump to convince his fellow-electors
that he knows all about politics, and he dreams
that they have nothing to do but listen to him
in order to be fully persuaded. Ask these men
to pray in public, to speak for Christ, to exhort
sinners to flee from the wrath to come, to invite
the penitent to come to Jesus; the majority of

them will become dumb, most of the rest will enter upon such work so reluctantly, that no person could possibly have any faith in their prayers, testimonies or exhortations.

The women, likewise, are not deficient in fluency, they are equally gifted, and many of them are eloquent. When a number of them meet on a social occasion they are at no loss for something to say. They can clothe their thoughts in language which fully expresses their ideas without any hesitation. They have a general knowledge and the subject-matter don't fail, it seems to be a fountain springing up, and at times it flows over. They are thoroughly conversant with the latest styles. The last cut has not escaped the glance of their keen eyes. Being so thoroughly posted, they are thereby qualified for able discussion, thorough investigation, and close logical conclusions. With an artistic finish of expression every sentence is uttered as though the salvation of the world depended upon their enunciation of the minutest details. They are nearly all fluent and eloquent, and with precise and clear-

3

cut statement they can express their thoughts
and feelings. It may be that a very large
majority of them are silent in the prayer-
meetings, if they attend. They can't pray.
They are not talented. They have never made
a habit of praying in public. Somebody else
can do it better. They can make an excuse of
some kind. They don't all speak in class and
fellowship meetings. Some of them don't believe in women speaking. They could tell you
very readily that the Bible says that it is a
shame for a woman to speak in church. They
would not try to harmonize their application of
this Scripture with other portions of God's
Word. Others say that it is not necessary to
speak, that God knows that they love Him.
Some who do speak are not heard. They turn
their faces away from their brethren and sisters.
Others close their eyes when bearing witness to
the blessed redemption. When an appeal is
made by the watchman in Israel, for consecrated workers around the altar of prayer, or
through the promiscuous congregation, many of
them remain in their pews unmoved. They

don't respond to the call. The preacher did
not mean that they should go. They are not
adapted for that kind of work. The preacher
should talk personally to the people himself.
They are not called to active service in the
Church. They can sit there and decay and die,
while the children of the Church go to hell by
the hundred. They are not concerned about
these things. They don't seem to know anything about the perishing. Oh! ye careless
daughters of Zion! How long! Will ye still
refuse to awake from your slumber? "Tremble,
ye women that are at ease; be troubled, ye careless ones; strip you and make you bare, and
gird sackcloth upon your loins."

In the human soul there are latent powers
that have been paralyzed by sin, which remain
dormant until they are brought into life by the
sanctifying energy of the Holy Ghost. When
they are brought fully into light and activity
they are not to be used for selfish purposes.
When God has given us the gift of pardon, the
assurance of faith, the witness of the Spirit,
heaven around, within, beyond, and above us,

and the light and cheering prospect of the enjoyment of that heaven forever, can we retain this blessedness and not let our brothers and sisters in Adam know anything about it ? Can a soul with this experience be at ease in Zion ? Nothing short of entire consecration to the service of God could possibly satisfy a soul thus blessed. He who creates, redeems and regenerates will accept of nothing less than the entire sanctification of body, soul and spirit. He has made known His will in this matter. His will must be accomplished in us before we can see His face in glory. Shall millions for whom Christ died drop into hell and your soul, saved and enjoying this blessedness, remain at ease ? Does it not appeal to all that is good in you for a practical consecration of yourself to God, to enter into active service for the salvation of the perishing ? The gifts which God has given us are to be used for His glory, and He has given us the Spirit, to set us on fire and fan us into a flame, to make us burning and shining lights. The gift which is not used cannot be developed, but must lose all its vital energy. Those who won't pray will lose their power to pray. Those who might teach, exhort, entreat, and plead with sinners to come to Christ, and fail to do so, will lose their love and zeal. A thorough, complete, full, and entire consecration of all the gifts that God has given, to be used everywhere for His glory, is the only antidote for backsliding. True, you may not backslide in life, but you will in heart. You may incessantly attend to private devotions, to the reading of the Scriptures, to family devotions, to the means of grace; but, unless you consecrate all your gifts to God, you will backslide in heart, and your profession of religion will only be an empty sound. The Church of Christ is not suffering from the want of men of learning, loyalty, liberalty or eloquence. What it needs most is consecrated members, who delight in spending their time in winning souls. There are many who can conduct a prayer-meeting to the edification and profit of all present. The Sabbath-schools are at no loss for teachers; the financial interests of the Church in general are not neglected, it is not difficult to secure faithful stewards.

But there is great and pressing need of such men as the apostles set apart in the churches; men full of the Holy Ghost and faith; men who will win souls for the Lord Jesus; men who will preach Christ on the market-place, on the highway, behind the counters, in the work-shops, in the saloons, in the gambling-hells, and are not afraid of men or devils. Men and women in the church who will not wait for sinⲧ ners to come and ask what they must do to be saved, but will follow them into the highways and hedges and compel them to come in and fill God's house. Many would go; perhaps you would if you could preach like Paul, if you could accomplish something to commence with which would startle a continent, but you are not willing to break down in your first attempt to work for Jesus. Your grammar might be faulty, your sentences might not have an artistic finish. Your thoughts might not be clothed in the most elegant language, and these probable occurrences would be a severe blow to your pride. The gift which is not consecrated and used will diminish. Every faculty which is not exercised will lose moral strength. Those gifts and faculties most vigorously used will be developed most. When the consecration is complete, and the work of sanctification in the body, soul and spirit is perfect, the natural and spontaneous outburst of the fire in the soul, fanned by the Holy Ghost, will be eloquence of the highest type, it will melt, move, and persuade.

CONSECRATED INFLUENCE.

Many positively declare that they have no influence. Are you one of that number? Might you not as well say, "I am nobody," as to say, "I have no influence?" When you write, sign your name, "Nobody," if you have no influence. You might as well say, "I am a cipher, and not a tangible existence at all." Do be something. Should some other person affirm that you were a mere cipher, that no person was influenced either for better or for worse on account of your existence, would you not immediately stand upon your dignity? Would you not assert your personality? Would you not wish it to be

understood that you were of some importance
and wielded some influence? If you are a
half-hearted professor of religion, claiming to be
a Christian, and identifying yourself with God's
people, when in reality you are a sinner, living
as worldly people live; talking as the ungodly
talk; acting as the openly profane; then you
are a stumbling-block, and sinners are tumbling
over you into hell. You have an influence. The
Lord Jesus decided this point. He said: "He
that gathereth not with Me scattereth abroad."
So, then, you are either leading the perishing to
the Lord Jesus, or you are helping the devil to
damn them in hell. Some persons are being
directly influenced by you, and are coming to
Christ seeking salvation; or, they are being
driven headlong on the "broad road that leadeth
to destruction," and finally, "where the worm
dieth not and the fire is not quenched." A certain infidel said that he did not believe in God,
that he did not believe in the Bible, that Christians were ignoramuses." He said that they
could not talk to him. An old father in Israel
said that he would talk with him. The time was

set, and the place appointed for the discussion.
They had a full house. The infidel had the first
privilege, and with much gush he exhausted
himself, giving vent to his blasphemy. Then
the old Christian man got on his feet. He
referred first to his conversion to God, which
followed his repentance toward God and faith
in the Lord Jesus Christ. He affirmed, with
much assurance, that God had saved him
through the atoning blood of His Son. The
Spirit of God had at that time come into his
heart and was there still. He said that he had
consecrated himself entirely to God, and He had
saved him fully and kept him. The blessing of
God rested upon the old man, as he witnessed a
good confession, telling redemption's story, and
the tears rolled down his cheeks. The audience
was fully persuaded, and wept with the old
veteran of the cross. The infidel became very
uneasy on his seat, then bowed his head in submission, and when it became too hot for him he
took his hat and started for the door. Some of
the audience called after him, and said that they
wanted to hear more from him. He replied to

them, "I can't stand this! I can't stand this! I can stand before any man, but I can't stand before God in a man." It has always been so, it is so at the present time, and it will be so until the end. Consecrated Christians are always full of God, and they are a terror to evil-doers. They are also a terror to half-hearted professors of religion; their zeal, earnestness, fervent prayers, and powerful testimonies incite a spirit of jealousy among formalists.

The authoritative father has a wonderful influence over his child, he can bring it up just as he pleases. Take, for example, the man who is consecrated to the devil. There are many of that class. Observe the influence he has over his child. Probably, the first word uttered by the child was an oath; from the common oath to blasphemy, to drinking, to dancing, to the card-table, to the bar-room, to the ball-room, to the theatre, and to the horse-race, until he is an expert in all vice. His father looks on him, and gloats over him out of his devilish soul, and exclaims, see my boy, how clever he is!

He is perfection in the eyes of his father. If men under the devil can thus form and fashion a life, what can fathers do who are consecrated to God and filled with the Holy Ghost? They can do what God has commanded. They can train up their children in the way they should go, and when they are old they shall not depart from it. They can bring them up in the fear and admonition of the Lord. Mothers should have a powerful influence over their children. They are so much in their presence. When young they are under their special care. In more mature years when about the home they are personally with them. Their eyes are upon them and they see all their movements. Mothers often forget that the eyes of their children are upon them, that they look straight through them. Children can tell pretty well how much religion their mothers possess. They know when their mothers pray with fervor, and they know better when they seldom pray and frequently scold. Children know when their mothers are full of the love of God, and the power of the Spirit. They know when they can't help but obey, the words being such, so much of a true mother's heart in them. They also know when their mothers' words are harsh, and their souls set on fire of hell. The children know when arrows have been driven into their souls, having escaped from their mothers' lips, which make them feel like being ugly. They know when their mothers' faces shine like the faces of angels, and they know when they look like the devil. Young men have a marvellous influence over each other. At a certain place where revival services were being held, among a number who were converted was a young man who had a very ungodly associate. When his companion heard of his conversion, he said that he would soon drive piety out of his head. With much assurance he said, just let me get talking to him. The county fair came off a few days later. He followed him incessantly all day; in the evening he succeeded in getting him into the hotel; then he forced him to the bar-room and caused him to drink.

The young man absented himself as quickly as possible from his company, and started on his

journey home. His companion armed himself
with a bottle of the inebriating drug, and pur-
sued his victim to accomplish his devilish design.
He went to the church where the services were
being held, and not finding him there, he retired
and proceeded to the young man's home, and
then to his bedside. He induced him again to
drink from the intoxicating cup, to pour distilled
damnation into his body, which had been dedicated to God to be a temple of the Holy Ghost.
He destroyed the young man's peace, severed
him from God, dragged him into the mud again,
arrested him a prisoner of darkness, a dupe of
the devil, and an heir of damnation. It is stu-
pendous what men can do and are accomplishing
for the devil. If these men were converted and
consecrated to God, how they could lift up
humanity! If those who have been converted
were consecrated, how they could reach their
companions, schoolmates, etc. If no man is truly
a man until he is fully the Lord's, then none
can know how much he can do, much less
accomplish it, until he is fully consecrated, and
the Lord has had an opportunity to develop his

powers and bring out all that there is in him. Young women have a marvellous influence in their homes. Are you a sister? If you are fully consecrated to God, you can influence your brother's mind, heart and will, and turn the whole tendency of his life. If you are a sister, then you are a daughter, and by the potency of your piety and earnestness, your father may be induced to reform. He may be so influenced by your life that it will be impossible for him to stifle conviction, seeing and being overcome by your loyalty to Christ, and your holiness in all manner of conversation. The laws of nature and of God being fulfilled, you will bear the honored name of wife, and the more sacred one of mother. Your influence will be a potent factor in determining the happiness or misery of your husband, and it will, without fail, fix the destiny of your children.

Moral influence is an ocean boundless as eternity. It is a powerful force either for good or evil among men. This power is inherent and universal; it clings to us; we can't shake it off, for it is imbedded in our nature and increases as we grow, either good or evil. It moves, walks, speaks, and there is no limit to its operations. It is potent in every look and act of our lives. We are necessarily either tempests to destroy humanity, or we are beacon lights to illumine life's pathway and thereby lead the wanderer in safety. It depends upon our own choice which we will accomplish. The following is the bitter wail of a dying man : " Oh, that my influence could be gathered up and buried with me!" That could not be. His influence survived him; it never dies; it works on ; it will run through all eternity. His body was shrouded and buried, but his influence will never be entombed; it is destined to live forever. The deadly work goes on when the man is silent in the tomb. It will walk the earth from pole to pole as a pestilence —like a destroying angel, carrying destruction and death in its train. The person consecrated to the devil will increase the weeping and wailing of millions of the damned in hell ; and the person fully consecrated to God, wields such an influence that millions of souls will have more joy, brighter crowns, greater mansions, fuller

apprehensions of God, greater treasures, and will
be more capable of enjoying God forever.

The greatest victories which have been
achieved, and the most wonderful works that
have been done for God, have not been accomplished by the hundreds or by large companies.
Reforms and revivals have been brought about
by single individual efforts. The person who
will dare to stand alone, who is so fully dedicated
to God that he can bear the frown of the world,
who will dare to oppose his best friend in the
Gospel, and will not be moved by friend or foe,
is the kind of character that God Almighty, in
every case, uses for His own glory. There were
many reformers, but there was only one Luther.
In every denomination there are multitudes of
communicants, but a very small fraction of the
number do all the practical work that is done in
the vineyard. There are many who have been
converted, but how comparatively few are
entirely consecrated to soul-winning. Many say
that they love Jesus, and are in sympathy with
Him in saving perishing humanity. How few
of that number demonstrate by their prayers,

exhortations, and practical efforts to lead sinners to Christ, that their profession is genuine ? If we would move men mightily for God, our souls must be surcharged with fire from heaven, so that all who come in contact with us, and those we seek after, shall feel the secret, silent, but omnipotent power of God proceeding from us. We must draw near to the source from whence the fire emanates, to the throne of God and the Lamb, and shut ourselves in from the world and its cold and chilling breezes. We must enter our closets and shut the doors, and there, isolated from the form, fashion and allurements of the world, wait before God for the holy anointing. God will come; He will not tarry. He will come speedily. He will baptize with the Holy Ghost. The promise cannot fail. The fire will come upon and go through us. We shall be anointed for service. Then we will go forth, not in our own strength, but in the demonstration of the Spirit and of power. Every person we meet, saint and sinner, will be moved by the power. There will be a fascination in the glance of the eye which will hold men spell-bound, and

4

make them feel that we have been with Jesus and learned of Him. Every tone of the voice will be full of spiritual magnetism, which will thrill any audience. Every prayer offered will shake the heavens and make the bottomless pit tremble. Every effort of faith will sound the depths of the multitude of unbelieving hearts around us.

We are living in the midst of a circle of friends and neighbors who are our schoolmates and associates. On their immortal minds we are making impressions, by our words and actions, which can never be effaced. We are instructing in the way of truth and righteousness; or we are diverting the mind from these things, and it will be reckoned for or against us at the judgment seat. Our influence is operating indirectly on people we have never seen or communicated with, as potently as on those in our immediate presence. There are men in our presence to-day who in a short time may be thousands of miles away repeating what we have said, spreading broadcast loose and unchaste expressions which may have fallen from our lips. Or they may catch the flame of our zeal and enthusiasm, and be led by it to consecration and holy living. They may spread scriptural holiness throughout the land, thousands of miles away from any point where our voices have been heard. "No human being can come into this world without increasing or diminishing the sum total of human happiness, not only for the present, but of every subsequent age of humanity. Thousands of my fellow-beings will yearly enter eternity with characters differing from those they would have carried thither had I never lived." It is a most solemn thing to have a being among our fellow-creatures. "Nothing that is said is ever extinguished, nothing that is done ever ceases its influence. It goes out from us, and is never arrested or put an end to. The pebble that I drop into the sea will send out its undulations forever and ever. The blow that I strike upon the earth will transmit its vibrations forever and ever. A word once said is repeating itself in the air till the judgment-day ; and Scripture leads us to infer that it will at that day meet us again, a memorial of the good or the evil we have done."

We are influenced, changed and modified by our environment. "Nothing leaves us wholly as it found us. Every man we meet, every book we read, every picture or landscape we see, every word or tone we hear, mingles with our being and modifies it." What is this influence which is within us and going out from us? It may be a tree sprung up from a root of bitterness, having many branches laden with corrupt fruit, and many thereby be defiled. Or it may be leaven, gradually fermenting and working into the whole mass for good. It may be a worldly spirit, which casts a repellant shadow over those who are seriously inclined, and drives those who may not be far from the kingdom into darkness and despair. Or it may be that full consecration of life and character, which magnetizes and draws men irresistibly to the cross of Christ, to find pardon, peace and salvation. It may be a spirit of pride, of conformity to the world, and at the same time professing not to be of this world; then it is a stumbling-block, a rock of offence, the strongest force the devil has at his disposal for driving souls into hell. Or it may be a spirit of love, such as possessed the heart of Andrew when he found his brother Simon and brought him to Jesus. It may be the spirit that imbued Nicodemus when he came to Jesus by night for fear of the Jews, which caused him after he had received instruction in the way of life, to keep it a secret, lest he should be cast out of the synagogue. Or it may be the Christ-like spirit of the woman of Samaria who, when she received the light did not put it under a bushel, but ran straightway and told the whole city that she had found the Messiah and brought them to Jesus. It may be a fearful, cowardly, recreant spirit, such as possessed the unfaithful spies, who confessed that it was a goodly land, but allowed themselves to be terrorized by the giants and spread demoralization and death throughout the camp of Israel. Or it may be the true, faithful, fearless, godly spirit which remained in Joshua and Caleb, which made them dare to stand alone and declare that they were well able to possess the land, and drive out all their enemies in the name of the Lord.

CONSECRATED PROPERTY.

The gold, silver, and cattle upon a thousand hills belong to God by absolute right. Are you one of that class of people who talk about their money, property, houses, cattle, etc., and mean just what you express in words? You would not care to be called a thief and a robber. Yet you are both in the true sense of the word, until you, without reserve, consecrate everything in your possession to God, the lawful owner. You own nothing; you never did, you never will in this world; you are only a steward. What you claim and call yours, belongs to God; and you never can be an honest sinner or a true Christian until you give up that which does not belong to you. Every inch of ground, every fraction of money, all goods and property, must be given to God, the deed must be drawn up in your own mind and heart, the pen of consecration must go into the ink, and the hand of faith must apply it to the paper. It is not enough to have your own name to the deed, you must see that God's name is stamped upon it, you must

have the King's seal. All this will not be sufficient; it is absolutely necessary for you to have
the Holy Ghost for a witness. The ground
having been entirely consecrated to the Lord, it
will be tilled for Him. Those who plough for
the Lord are as fully blessed and are as happy
as those who are in the pulpit preaching the
Gospel of Christ. What is true of the consecrated tiller of the ground is true of all men in
their varied callings. The consecrated farmer
sows the seed, when the soil is prepared, for the
Lord. If it buds, grows and blossoms, the immediate causes are the sunshine, the rain and
the dews, together with the general adaptation
of the climate, which are absolutely controlled
by God. He may send torrents of rain and
wash and flood it out of the ground, and the
prospect for a harvest may be as gloomy as if
the ground had not been prepared or the seed
sown. Or He may cause it to grow until the
ground is covered and the hills are waving in
grain; and then He may send a drouth, and
burn it off close to the ground, and labor is
seemingly lost and the prospect for a harvest

removed. He may send showers, sunshine and dews, causing it to shoot and present the full corn in the ear; and then He may blast it until it is fit only to be trodden under foot.

Those who are not entirely consecrated to God would not have the place deluged with water. When everything is parched and dry, if they had control they would bring showers of rain. If God would permit them to control the clouds for a short time they would show the Omniscient how to control the weather. They murmur and find fault, they keep themselves and all who listen to them in misery. It don't prevent the rain from falling, neither does it bring the shower when they desire it. Those who have completed their consecration can praise God in the rain, when general destruction is being produced by the torrents of water flooding and deluging the whole country, just the same as when showers are more moderate and causing everything to bud and blossom. They can praise God when the ground is dry and parched, when everything is withering under the scorching rays of the burning sun. Praise is the spontaneous outcome of the soul in perfect harmony with God. When the Lord gives, it is praise, and when He taketh away, it is blessed be the name of the Lord. " The bread and the water will not fail " having become the language of the heart, there is no disposition to dictate the ways and means by which they are to come, or the channel through which they must pass, it is enough that He has promised The consecrated soul confides in God and asks no questions. There is to him a never-failing stream from the promise that " all things work together for good to them that love God." He became convinced that God would accept him and fulfil all His promises in his experience, and consecrated all, reserving nothing to trouble him. Having learned that it was his privilege, he consecrated all, both small and great. That which is not consecrated will in every case give trouble. When horses die, the loss drives praise and thanksgiving out of some men, their faces literally become long, a gloom is cast over their lives for some days, if not for weeks, they fret, worry and complain, and want to know why they have such bad luck. The following questions are not generally asked: Did I use him well when I had him? Did I feed him well? Did I never drive him when he was thirsty? Did I not often drive him too fast? Was he mine? Did he not belong to the Lord? Did I beat him when I should not have done so? Is it not cruel to beat dumb animals? Have I killed the Lord's horse? Consecration is incomplete until the horses are given to the Lord and the labor they perform. When horses commence to work for the Lord, it will be a wonderful relief to them, it will save their bones from many bruises, and their hides from many severe lashes. They will be fed more regular. The drives will become much shorter. The speed will be modified, and they will not be abused in any way. God must have the gold. Every mite must be given. It is not enough to give so much on the first day of the week. That which is not set apart for the advancement of His cause must be given, either to take away from us or leave in our possession as He pleases. If God requires to use it all, it must be at His disposal.

The consecrated man can give a million as freely as one dollar. Should he be worth hundreds of millions and God were to take away from him the last mite for the advancement of His cause, he can praise God as freely as the woman who cast in her two mites. He is ready to get on his knees and break stones for a living ; if not, he is not entirely consecrated to God's service. The consecrated man gives of his means all that God requires of him. He gives it in the right spirit, at the right time, and in the right place. There is no such thing as begging from consecrated people. All they require to know is the special need from the different sources. They give according as God would have them dispose of the means in their possession. They never give grudgingly, for God loveth a cheerful giver. It is their joy to make their plans, and all their calculations, to bring the most possible glory to God, by sustaining His cause, helping His people, and supporting the ministry of the word. Many of the professed followers of the Lord Jesus don't give in this way. The ministers of Jesus Christ who have the cause at heart, send the most hopeful to collect for the cause of missions, and the millions of the perishing. They enter into their appointed work full of expectation, calling upon God's people to aid His cause by contributing of their means. They go to the home of a man who prays long and loud, and occupies the greater part of ten minutes to relate his experience of God's saving power in his soul, and he scarcely knows at times whether he is in or out of the body. He don't seem to have the cause of missions at heart, for some reason unknown to men and angels. He did not know that the collectors would call upon him that day, or he would not have been at home. He submits to the inevitable, and at once resolves to make a desperate effort to save himself by framing excuses, and resorts to finding fault with preachers, missionaries, the expenditure of moneys, and everything is wrong from first to last. He wants to know what has been done with all the money which has been given. He positively affirms that he could have evangelized the whole world with what has been spent already. He declares that those who handle the money are only a company of rogues, that they pocket most of it; indeed, if they had to earn it as he had to do, they would know where it came from. They can step around in their broadcloth, while he has to take off his coat and earn a living. They drive their fast horses and covered carriages, while he walks to most places to do business. Their families live higher, and carry higher heads than he is able to afford about his house. He commences to feel that his anger is taking the form of wrath, and it would be better not to let the sun go down before he becomes calmer and somewhat placid.

Then he resorts to another method of defence, lest he should be induced to be somewhat liberal, and he commences to trifle with the un-sullied motives of the collectors. He wants to know if they would not rather enter the matri-monial state than collect missionary money, and dares to insinuate that they are on the look-out. After resorting to every means to fortify himself—as scolding, slander, insinuation, fault-finding and jeering—he sends them away with as little as possible. He compliments himself for his shrewdness and cleverness in getting rid of them so easily. Hear, O ye heavens, and give ear, O earth! Is this what it is to be clever and shrewd? Is this the way that ten hundred and thirty millions of our lost race are going to hear the Gospel of Christ? Is this the religion of our Lord and Saviour Jesus Christ? Is this consecration to God and allegiance to Christ? Is it the spirit which imbued apostles, martyrs, and our fathers in the Gospel? It is perverted formalism, which has not even the semblance of the religion of Christ.

All unconsecrated means, property, and wealth is stamped with robbery, ruination and damnation. The possessor will have trouble and disquietude. He will have a conscious fear of the judgment. That which is withheld can only prove a curse, it will bring leanness upon the soul and finally eternal separation from God. "The treasures we withhold are moth-eaten; the sacrifice which we do not present on the divine altar becomes a stench; the choice things reserved to ourselves are transmuted into curses;

the incense which we do not offer to Jesus
ministers to self-love, vanity, and idol-worship ;
the disloyalty and treason to heaven's king
produce anarchy, misery, and a dreary desola-
tion and darkness of death in the soul."

Everything that we deliberately and wilfully
withhold from God, is not only a perpetual
curse to our own souls, but is also a blighting
and blasting influence upon the rising generation.   The full, complete consecration of everything in our possession to God is the only
possible way of preventing these things from
having an undue influence and power over us.
A good man when asked how he gave so much,
replied, " The Lord is all the time shovelling it
on me, and I would be overwhelmed if I did not
give."   The Lord gives wealth, and when it is
not dedicated by the recipient for God's glory,
he is buried beneath it as under an avalanche of
ruin.

When the heart is fixed on God, the love
becomes intense, and the soul longs to have
more to give.   Mary, who loved the Saviour so
much, did not think that the ointment was too

costly to be used on Him. Our Father does not look for the best of our substance; He claims His right, that is all. He giveth all things richly to be enjoyed, and loveth a cheerful giver. He giveth not best who giveth most, but he giveth most who giveth best. He that giveth willingly giveth well.

"The moon is a great giver, and she owes all her beauty to this habit of giving. Suppose the moon should swallow up and keep to itself all the rays of light which the sun gives it and should refuse to give them to us, what would the effect be ? It would stop shining. And the moment it would stop shining, it would lose all its beauty. If it should stop shining or giving away the light it gets from the sun, it would hang up in the sky a great, black, ugly-looking ball. All its brightness and beauty would be gone."

"It is more blessed to give than to receive." Consecration makes giving not a duty incumbent upon us, which must be attended to at the peril of our souls, but a blessed privilege, a supreme delight, the joy of the heart, and a means of grace. Men who are entirely consecrated take hold of the financial interests of God's cause, and press them as they do all other business transactions.

"The Church will never realize her full measure of prosperity till her wealthy and cultured laymen take hold of her enterprises of beneficence, as they take hold of bank and railroad enterprises, putting themselves into them with all their resources of energy and capital, resolved to make them a success."

The Old Testament teaching regarding property and possessions is that all should be consecrated to God, and one-tenth given into the treasury for the special work of the Church. With the increase of light, liberty and blessings, there should be an increase in giving, in order that this blessedness might be the common privilege of all the human family.

"Ye are a chosen generation, a royal priesthood, a holy nation, a peculiar people, that ye should show forth the praises of Him who hath called you out of darkness into His marvellous light."

5

Should we not, then, follow one of John Wesley's golden rules and make all we can, save all we can, and give all we can?

"Jay Cooke, of Philadelphia, early in his life, read 'Gold and the Gospel,' and resolved to take Jacob's pledge. 'Of all that Thou shalt give me, I will surely give the tenth unto Thee.' He directed his clerk to open an account with O. P. J. (Old Patriarch Jacob) and to credit to it one-tenth of all the commissions that came into the office. Some of the largest financial transactions of the country were entrusted to the firm of which he was a member, and its success was one of the wonders of the land. O. P. J.'s account amounted to a sum that would take the figures of five places to express. When asked how he could afford to give such large contributions, he said, 'It don't cost me anything; it's the Lord's money, I give.'"

It has not been left optional with us whether we support God's cause or not. The commands, exhortations and instructions are clear and explicit.

"Charge them that are rich in this world,

that they be not high-minded, nor trust in uncertain riches, but in the living God, who giveth us richly all things to enjoy; that they do good, that they be rich in good works, ready to distribute, willing to communicate; laying up in store for themselves a good foundation against the time to come, that they may lay hold on eternal life."

A most solemn charge, a forcible exhortation to humility, a warning against the deceitfulness of riches, and a plain, clear statement of how distributions should be made by those who are the possessors of wealth. God hath commanded, exhorted, and made it binding on the poor to give of their means. He has commended those who gave all their living. We may be poor and yet make many rich. "The poor shall not give less than half a shekel, when they give an offering to the Lord." That would be over four dollars, and that would purchase nearly ten times as much as the same nominal sum now. Then, unless God required more from His people who had less light than He gives at the present,

the poor now should give not less than forty
dollars when making an offering to the Lord.
Lady Maxwell said that God had taught her
not only that her conveniences must give way
to other people's necessities, but also her necessities to other people's extremities.

A letter was received, and on the inside of
the envelope, which contained six penny stamps
and nothing else, the following words were
written : " Fasted a meal to give a meal." What
is required is the diligent and faithful labors,
tears, sacrifices, and offerings of men and
women, to build God's spiritual Zion, and support her against all the encroachments of earth
and hell combined. "And they came both men
and women, as many as were willing-hearted,
and brought bracelets, and ear-rings, and rings,
and tablets, all jewels of gold ; and every man
that offered, offered an offering of gold unto the
Lord. And all the women that were wise-
hearted did spin with their hands, and brought
that which they did spin, both of blue, and of
purple, and of scarlet, and of fine linen."

" Whate'er our willing hands can give,
    Lord, at Thy feet we lay ;
  Grace will the humble gift receive,
    And grace at length repay."

CONSECRATED TIME.

The consecration of every moment of time to
God does not mean that we must leave home,
friends and business to preach the Gospel in
foreign lands, or on domestic missions, but it
does mean that we are willing to do that or anything else that God requires us to do.   In every
case it means that we are to preach.   Every
Christian is a preacher.   There is the universal,
as well as the special, call to preach.   All who
are converted are called in that general sense.
They are called, set apart, and sealed for the
work.   " The Spirit and the Bride say, Come ;
and let him that heareth say, Come."   " And the
inhabitants of one city shall go to another, saying, Let us go speedily to pray before the Lord,
and to seek the Lord of hosts ; I will go also."
The Gospel come and the Gospel go are inseparable.   Those who have accepted the invitation
and have found salvation through the atoning

blood of the Lord Jesus, will go out to seek, find
and bring back the wanderers to the fold of
Christ. "'Tis all their business here below to
cry, Behold the Lamb!" Andrew found Peter
and brought him to Jesus. Philip findeth
Nathanael, and said to him, "Come and see,"
and he came to Jesus. The language of the
new-born soul is,

> "O that the world might taste and see
> The riches of His grace."

Every moment should be consecrated to God in
active service : " Take my moments." Time is
the gift of God, and He gives one moment at a
time, without any promise that another will
succeed it. The fully consecrated soul lives by
the moment, acts on the moment, and is ready
to do each moment that which he finds to do.
Time seems to be too short for the consecrated
soul, the moments go like a flash, while the work
is pressing, and the borders are being enlarged.
The golden opportunities for achieving blessed
victories for the cause of Christ become too
limited. Life seems to be but a moment, and
the harvest fields, white with the golden grain,

would require an age for reaping. " The harvest truly is great and the laborers are few."
Through consecration we learn the value of a
moment of time; when the worth of a thing has
been realized, the thing itself can be properly
estimated. We learn that a marvellous work
can be accomplished in a short time, when the
soul is so fully dedicated that God can have all
His own way. We learn, also, that God has
His own time for doing His work, and that time
can be known only to the consecrated, who keep
themselves in harmony with the divine mind.
And we learn, also, that God's work must be
done at the present moment, that His time is
now, not in the indefinite future. We are living
epistles, and we are read, known and imitated
by many with whom we associate. Saints and
sinners are not only preaching, but leaving their
impress upon humanity. The children of God
are to bear holy fruit, the end of which is to be
everlasting life.

They are the light of the world, and are
expected to shine and never grow dim. Their
lights are not to be under a bushel, but they are

to shine, every moment, in every place; on the house-top, on the market-square, on the public road, on the political platform; in business transactions, in honest dealing, in paying all lawful debts, in the darkest corners, in the clear light, in the prayer-meeting, in the fellowship-meeting; under severe temptations, under the most bitter persecution, under trial and tribulation; at the stake, at the cross, at the block; even to death. The lower lights are to be kept burning, and sending their beams across the waves.

John the Baptist was a burning and a shining light. The Christian selects his text every morning, enters into it, analyzes and expounds it. Just as the wheel of time ushers him into the duties, privileges and perplexities of the day. The introduction and exegesis is generally interesting and edifying. Secret prayer before leaving the bed-chamber is generally entered into with a good deal of fervency, in this way the text for the day is chosen, analyzed and digested. Family worship is performed with sincerity, devotion, and apparently with full

submission. The first part of the sermon for
the day is genuine and orthodox, sound in scriptural exposition, and practical in all its bearings.
Those who listen could not be otherwise than
favorably impressed. The face of the preacher
is aglow with the light and love spontaneously
bursting forth from the soul illuminating the
place, and causing those present to feel that it
was good indeed to be there. The whole day is
not spent in these delightful and profitable
exercises, there are other duties devolving upon
the preacher, and he must go on with the next
division of his discourse. It assumes a more
practical bearing, and it becomes a little more
difficult to keep to the text. His face don't
shine with such brilliancy, the rhetorical flow of
language is somewhat impeded, his theology is
become corrupted, quotations are not scriptural,
and the wanderings from the text more frequent and discernible.

Sermons from the pulpit are frequently criticised, and most severely, when they have not a
rhetorical and oratorical finish, notwithstanding
the preacher is earnestly enforcing the plain

Gospel of Christ, as a faithful minister of Jesus Christ. When the sermons preached by the congregation, in the market-places, behind the counters, in the harvest-fields, and among the horses and cattle, are as scriptural and true to the whole Word of God as those delivered from the pulpit, we will have revivals which will not be spasmodic, but will extend through the years, growing brighter and deeper, until the whole world will bow at the feet of Jesus, and crown Him Lord of all. When the day is commenced with fervent prayer and supplication, and many outbursts of anger interspersed throughout the hours of the day, the mixture is unwholesome, and leads only to confusion, darkness and damnation. In the prayer-meeting praying with zeal, force, and seemingly with power; in the love-feast soaring, and apparently having need of nothing only the wings in order to be translated immediately without either a chariot or a legion of angels; on the way home attacked, pressed, crossed, severely tried until riled, then an outburst of anger, and the angel-like appearance having disappeared, he looks like a personified devil.

Reader, is that what you would call consecration? Christians who are consecrated to God don't wander from, but stick to, the text, and under provocation and temptation they pray more and preach better. They go through every division of the sermon with the same, only an increase of fervor and enthusiasm. They drive home the truth wherever the occasion permits. They give clear expositions of Scripture, close exegesis, and a practical application. Their conversations are seasoned with grace, and every speech is sound and cannot be condemned. When they are required to make the application of their discourses, and that is the trying time, they rise equal to the occasion. They are always true to their Master. They are in the front of the ranks, to stand or fall in pushing the battle to the gate. Every hour of our lives, every precious moment of time which God permits us to enjoy, is the purchased right of the Lord Jesus Christ. He received into His sacred bosom all the arrows of sin; He poured out His soul in sorrow, agony and blood, even unto death, to buy this time for us. Shall we squander these most golden hours, and not improve them, seeing they come as angels of love and mercy ? God forbid. The Lord help us, that we may consecrate them and use them for the glory of Him who died, and purchased them with His own blood.

What is time ? Plato said that time is a movable image of eternity, or the interval of the world's motion. Another writer hath said that it is the only thing that we can innocently be covetous of, and yet there is nothing of which we are more lavishly and profusely prodigal. The moment that is lost is gone forever. It can't be recalled, and connected with it was an opportunity for doing good, which if ever is done must take the time and place of some other duty. A woman in great agony and despairing of mercy cried out to those who were endeavoring to comfort her, "Call back time again! If you can call back time again, then there may be hope for me; but time is gone." Queen Elizabeth said, "Millions of money for an inch of time!" Time is seldom properly estimated until the privilege it afforded has passed by us,

then in bitterness of despair we mourn our loss.
A devout man when he would hear the clock
strike would say, " Here is one hour past that I
have to answer for." As time is exceedingly
precious, so it is extremely short. It is swift on
wing and is suddenly gone. John Bradford
used to say, " I count that hour lost in which I
have done no good by my pen or tongue." How
time is lost! Lost, yesterday, somewhere between sunrise and sunset, two golden hours,
each set with sixty diamond minutes. No
reward is offered, for they have gone forever.
It is so easy for persons who are not entirely
consecrated to God to let the valuable moments
pass, without accomplishing anything in the
vineyard of the Lord.

The path of consecration and duty is the only
safeguard. When we are on duty the moments
seem too short, there are so many opportunities
for doing good. If we are not actively engaged
in supplying the need of urgent cases, we can
be preparing to supply others who are destitute.
Oh, the value of time ! Would that we could
realize its true worth before it is too late ! An

officer in the army apologized for a little delay,
" Only a few moments." General Mitchell replied, " I have been in the habit of calculating
the value of the one-thousandth part of a
second." How much could be added to our
lives if we would utilize all our time. How
many hours are heedlessly spent in bed. It is
good to have plenty of sleep and rest, but any
more than is absolutely necessary is time lost.
The difference between rising at five and seven
o'clock in the morning, for the space of forty
years, supposing a man to go to bed at the same
hour at night, is equivalent to the addition of
ten years to a man's life. This precious gift is
bestowed upon us to be improved, not in part,
but every moment. Every hour of the day,
every moment is a talent of time, and God expects the very best possible use to be made of it,
and will condemn the non-improvement of it in
the last day. How many would work for Jesus
if they only had time, but they have so many
things to look after, so much business to attend
to, they cannot possibly spare the time. They
have wilfully placed themselves in such a posi-

tion that their business demands even the moments. Their sympathies are not with the Christ in the salvation of the perishing, but with their own financial matters. Oh, the uncertainty of time! What is life? It is but a vapor. A few hours broken off the eternity of the future and immediately attached to the eternity of the past, during which what we accomplish will fix and seal our eternal destinies. A certain minister urgently requested a lady to engage in active work for Christ, to which he thought her specially adapted. She declined, saying, "My stay here will be probably too short to be of use; I do not know that I shall be here three months." He answered her, "I do not know that I shall be here one." She keenly felt his reproof, and accepted the proffered duty.

Time is passing rapidly. The moments are on the wing, and we are being hurried into eternity. We are meeting death on the way, and how soon we will be in its grasp. The struggle will not be long; we are destined to succumb. From death to judgment, to receive the things done in our bodies according to that we have done, to be judged out of our own mouths, to have measured to us as we have dispensed to others. To become fully cognizant of the time we have lost, and to hear the sentence passed upon them who did not feed the hungry, clothe the naked, visit the sick and those who were in prison. We are not going to judgment alone. All around us are those who have made no preparation for death, who have not set their houses in order. They are already in the shades of eternal night, blinded by the god of this world, strangers to the covenant of promise, without God, and without one ray of hope of heaven. What a field for labor! What an opportunity for practical work! A special demand for every spare moment of time, to rescue the perishing, care for the dying, and snatch them in pity as brands from a burning hell. Who will work? Who will devote time to this pressing need? All who have their eyes open. Such a sight will engender sympathy, beget love, create zeal and develop such a hungering and thirsting for the salvation of souls as will lead to practical and effectual efforts. Every moment that can possibly be utilized for this work will be given with pleasure by those who are entirely consecrated. Time! Time! Time! Oh, for time to accomplish something, and power to do it speedily. Father of lights, illuminate our pathway and make it plain. Saviour of mankind, make us like unto Thyself, that all our moments may be consecrated to this work. Holy Ghost, the Comforter, with all Thy gifts of power, inspire and quicken us for the work. Angels of mercy, assist us. Men, brethren, sisters and children, join us in this work; time is short, souls are precious, they are dying and being damned.

CONSECRATED REPUTATION.

There is nothing that troubles Christians more than what people may think or say about them. What will such a person think about it? What will they say, any way? These are questions which are asked more frequently than, What will God say? This man-fearing spirit is a power which will counteract the best

energies of God's people. It will destroy the
most persistent effort of any soul. It will divert
the mind, limit the faith, and in many cases make
duty a burden. Closely allied with this spirit
is what is known as a man-pleasing spirit, which
accompanies it in all the public means of grace.
There is no work that we undertake for God.
and souls, that would not be prosecuted in some
other way by our brethren and sisters in Christ.
Many of them would not pray so loud as you
do, and others would launch out freely and use
all their volume of voice for God's glory. Some
of them would not get excited as you do, according to their ideas of things, and others would
wax warmer and move the place. Those who
do not pray so loud as you do will not hesitate
to tell you that you make too much noise. The
probabilities are that they very seldom pray,
and one hundred such Christians would not
pray a soul into the kingdom in a generation.
They will tell you that God is not deaf, but they
will not quote to you that Jesus cried with a
loud voice. This will be a great trial for you,
especially when you consider that you have

been endeavoring to please them. When you are full of the love of God, and feel like praying and working for the salvation of all within your reach, and one of the best friends you have will tell you that you will cool off shortly, that he was excited once himself, but could see things differently now, it will be such a trial for you that you will very likely become discouraged, and tone down a little to please the formalist. Some of the best people you have known, whose profession of religion you have never questioned, will be horrified if your face is not always extremely long, if you don't appear as solemn as death, or if you should laugh in time of worship. They will not hesitate to lecture you, and declare to you that you are doing much harm. It will be a testing time for your faith in God. They may know more in a general way about the Word of God than you do. They don't know, and perhaps they do not wish to be told, that Sarah said, " God hath made me to laugh, so that all that hear will laugh with me." They have no place in their creed for the hysterical fits that David and all

Israel were subject to when the Lord turned the captivity of Zion. " Then was our mouth filled with laughter, and our tongue with singing ; then said they among the heathen, The Lord hath done great things for them, The Lord hath done great things for them, whereof they are glad."

Some Christians in the nineteenth century will not recognize what the heathen saw, and glorified God for revealing. The Saviour's blessing in that form they exclude, notwithstanding it is one of the beatitudes. " Blessed are ye that weep now, for ye shall laugh." Should God pour out His spirit upon you in such rich effusion that your body would sink under the weight of the divine glory, the very best men you are acquainted with, perhaps your spiritual adviser, would be greatly alarmed, and try to persuade you that you excited yourself too much, or your physical system was run down. And should God favor you again with another manifestation of His glory, perhaps all the friends you have would feel disgraced, and all your previous efforts to please completely

destroyed by the breath of His mouth. They
would deprive you of all the means of grace, if
possible, in order that you would become sane,
and your mind return to its normal condition,
which generally means a condition of partial or
absolute indifference. The history of the hiding
of Moses in the rock, while God was passing by,
seems to be adapted for a different age, and for
a particular purpose. Moses had a right to see
the glory, but men will tell us that we are not
to expect such things. Jesus said, " The glory
which Thou gavest Me I have given them."
Daniel's experience is brought up for discussion.
Oh, he was an inspired man for a purpose !
" Therefore I was left alone and saw this great
vision, and there remained no strength in me ;
for my comeliness was turned in me into cor-
ruption, and I retained no strength." Oh, his
was a peculiar case. We are not to expect such
things now. Why ? Are we living in a darker
age ? Has God hidden Himself from His
people ? Shall we not see greater things in this
nineteenth century of the Gospel dispensation,
than ever has been seen ? Was Solomon's

prayer inspired by God ? Did the fire not come down from heaven ? Or, did the priests and people get excited and imagine that this had all happened ? "And the priests could not enter into the house of the Lord, because the glory of the Lord had filled the Lord's house." Then was it the glory of the Lord or was it something else ? Oh, this was in olden times! "And when all the children of Israel saw how the fire came down, and the glory of the Lord upon the house, they bowed themselves with their faces to the ground upon the pavement, and worshipped, and praised the Lord, saying, For He is good; for His mercy endureth forever." Were the children of Isrsel excited or were they truly worshipping God ? Did they not see the fire ? Had they their faces on the pavement as God hath said, or must we accept the interpretation of those who bitterly oppose this manifestation of God's mercy and power ?

Saul of Tarsus fell down on the road while on his journey to Damascus. "And as he journeyed, he came near Damascus: and suddenly there shined round about him a light

from heaven; and he fell to the earth, and heard
a voice saying unto him: Saul, Saul, why perse-
cutest thou Me?" Did he not fall to the earth?
Did the light not suddenly shine round about
him from heaven? Yes, but he was a chosen
vessel. He was called to do a special work,
and being a man with a very strong will, it
required a miracle to convert him. Well, then,
when he was converted, what about the other
miracle in Jerusalem? "And it came to pass
that when I was come again to Jerusalem, even
while I prayed in the temple, I was in a trance."
How can this miracle be accounted for? Who
is responsible for it? Was he in a trance, or
was he just in an ecstasy? What would you
gain by this interpretation? If a miracle, as
you may call it, had to be performed to get
Paul converted, on account of his strong will,
what part of the man had to be broken by this
manifestation of miraculous power? Then he
was caught up into the third heaven and heard
things which was not possible to utter, and was
so ecstatic that he did not know whether he
was in the body or out of it; and his body was

so paralyzed by it, that ever after his bodily
presence was weak and his speech contemptible.
By what law in philosophy do you explain this,
or would you resort to crying out excitement,
hysteria, etc., to appease your troubled conscience? Peter was up on the housetop praying
and fell into a trance. "And he became very
hungry, and would have eaten; but while they
made ready, he fell into a trance." How do
you explain this? Oh, he got hungry and
fainted. He was always excitable and went
beyond his strength. Then how connect it with
his visit to Cornelius, the vision fulfilled, and
the Gentiles accepted?

We are adopted into God's family, not to
please the Church, not to please formalists, not
to please the world, not to please the sinner,
but to please God. We are to please God, not
in prayer, not in speaking, not in exhortation,
not in preaching, not in rejoicing, not in shouting, but in humble submission to His righteous
will, to obey Him at any cost. When we try to
please the world, the sinner, the formalist, the
saint, we displease God. Our reputations are at

stake. The only way to avoid being troubled about our characters is to consecrate them to God. Should we attempt to look after them we will naturally expect people to think and speak well of us, and it is certain they will not do that if we please God. Some who should sympathize, who should be most loyal to us, will in all probability be the first to speak lightly of us in our absence. When God has the keeping of our reputations, and we are fully persuaded in our own minds as to His ability, then our fretting and worrying ceases. Men may say all manner of evil against us falsely because we are entirely the Lord's, nevertheless we rejoice and are exceeding glad.

It will no longer be a cross to pray in public. It will be easy to pray. Having no reputation to look after, we can direct our petitions to God; and not having to think about how the audience may be commenting on them, we are prepared to believe for and receive the answer to the prayers. It will be our good pleasure to work for Jesus, not caring what others may think or say about us. If they approve, it will be all right; if they oppose it will make no difference to us. When God fills our mouths with laughter we will not quench the Spirit in order to please the people. When He makes us feel like shouting, we will not suppress our feelings on account of opposition from formalists. When He overcomes us with a mighty baptism of His Spirit, so that we fall and there remains no strength in us, as Daniel and Paul, we will not feel mortified over it.

CONSECRATED MEMORY.

The memory is that faculty of the mind which retains a knowledge of previous events, thoughts and ideas. The number who make a special effort to have the memory entirely dedicated to God in consecration is comparatively small. Most people never take the matter into consideration, and see or feel no necessity for having the memory consecrated. There is no faculty of the mind that requires more help. It needs to be prompted, inspired and developed by the operation of the Holy Spirit, in order to effectually grasp and retain the sublimest thoughts that may be presented. Thoughts that have not yet been fully grasped and vigorously held by the mind cannot be clearly and forcibly presented to the minds of others.

Many of the sins which are committed are the result of sluggish memories. If this faculty of the mind were active it would prevent many indulgences. The study of the Scriptures is not, as a usual thing, wilfully neglected, but in most cases forgotten. Many sins are the natural result of neglected duty, and duty would not be omitted if the memories were consecrated and quickened mightily by the Spirit. If the sad consequences of duty neglected—the condemnation, guilt and remorse of conscience—if these were held vigorously before the mind by a retentive memory, they would prove strong incentives to faithfulness, and save the mind from much distress and self-reproach. The children of Israel did evil in the sight of the Lord, when they forgot their miraculous deliverance out of the hands of Pharaoh, the dividing of the waters and passage through the

Red Sea, the cloud by day and the fire by night. They made the golden calf and worshipped it. When the mercy, the love, the kindness, the works, the gift of God's Son, and the salvation through the atoning blood, are not kept vividly before the mind, the soul will invariably fall into sin. When these are kept forcibly impressed upon the mind, the soul rises preeminently above the world and sin, and becomes healthy, active and powerful. The soul will know nothing only victory all along the line. The children of Israel were commanded to remember the way in which the Lord had led them. The remembrance of these things kept them humbled, and their trust in God became firmer. They never wandered after strange gods until they forgot the goodness and mercy of God. When the Psalmist sat by the rivers of Babylon and remembered Zion and wept, his soul was deeply moved. The memory being active, the heart is touched, the sympathies are deeply moved, and love becomes so intensified that it prompts to action. When we think there are many things to mourn over, when we call to rememberance the destitute, the afflicted, the lost, our souls will be so deeply moved, that it will be impossible to remain passive. The chief butler forgot Joseph. How many are forgotten who ought to be remembered, who are worthy of our kindest attention, who are in distress and need, who are perishing for lack of knowledge, who are captivated by the devil at his will, who are bound and utterly helpless ? " Let them be before the Lord continually, that He may cut off the memory of them from the earth, because that he remembered not to show mercy."

The sin of not showing mercy to the poor and destitute is such that our memories should be charged with the responsibility of looking for opportunities to do good and communicate. The command is, " Remember, therefore, how thou hast received." David remembered God in the night-watches, upon his bed, and his soul was comforted and strengthened. " And it shall be to you a fringe that ye may look upon upon it, and remember all the commandments of the Lord and do them." The Lord gave this command to Moses for the people, they were to make fringes on the borders of their garments, and on this fringe they were to put a blue ribbon, to keep their memories on the commandments of God, lest they should break them and thereby bring divine displeasure upon themselves, and sin and death among the chosen people. God gave to His ancient people, the Jews, these outward and visible reminders, so that the sense of sight could help the memory. By these helps the commandments of God were remembered and could be strictly obeyed. Under the new and more glorious dispensation the promptings and helps are not given through the senses, but through the knowledge of the Word, as imparted by the inspiration and illumination of the Holy Ghost. The Holy Ghost was not given to absolutely guide in all thinking, reading, worship and business transactions. He was not given to take the place of any faculty of the soul or mind, but to help them all. He came to inspire the highest motives, the loftiest sentiments, the remaining good in the human soul. He does not work independent of us, but He works in, through and by us. His operations are not apart from the written revelation unless in particular cases. Where there is no knowledge of the Word imparted to the intellect, He cannot use the written truth and works through nature. "The Gentiles which have not the law do by nature the things contained in the law." He reproves the world of sin, of righteousness, and of judgment. He enlightens, regenerates, and completes the work of sanctification. He reveals the truth and brings all things to remembrance that Jesus said—He helps the memory. The Lord Jesus said many things to His disciples which they did not understand at the time. It was the special work of the Holy Ghost to give them power to see and know what Jesus meant in every case that was mysterious to them. This was not done until Jesus was glorified and the fulness of the Spirit's dispensation had come. "These things understood not His disciples at the first: but when Jesus was glorified, then remembered they that these things were written of Him, and that they had done these things unto Him." Jesus had promised that the Father would send the Comforter to inspire, strengthen, and give them power to remember and understand. "But the Comforter, which is the Holy Ghost, whom the Father will send in My name, He shall teach you all things, and bring all things to your remembrance whatsoever I have said unto you." This should not be confounded with the special inspiration given to some of the apostles for the special work of writing the New Testament. There is a vast difference between the work of the Spirit in unfolding that which has already been given to the Church of God, and revealing to the mind that which men have never known or heard. The first is universal, the common privilege of all the sons and daughters of God, the second is special through the individual for the benefit of all.

The Holy Spirit does a work for and in us which is varied and most blessed. This one of helping the memory is special and very important. He restores to the memory truths and facts which are so obliterated that their reproduction is impossible, unassisted by Him.

This faculty of the mind should be entirely consecrated to God in the minutest details, there being so many things consequent upon its activity at the right time and place. If it is kept under the direct operations of the Spirit, it will be developed and become quick, shrewd and powerful. Under His melting and moulding energy the memory will become sensitive to the needs of others in straitened circumstances around us; clear and acute to call up at once the best method of adapting ourselves to their circumstances, and practical in adjusting our means for the accomplishment of the most possible good. In prayer and supplication, He indites the petitions, inspires the faith, draws out the memory after individual cases and their necessities, and assists the memory in getting hold of the promises for a basis for the faith. In speaking, He quickens the memory, inspires the thought, gives energy and power to the expression, and conveys to the heart that which is adapted. Those who thoroughly prepare and then depend entirely upon the Spirit are irresistible. When the memory is completely under

7

the control of the Spirit, words will flow with
ease and rapidity, the power of expression will
become elastic, and all is in order without any
effort or anxiety. We must not suppose that
we are not to be thoughtful and studious. The
Spirit never makes up for any neglect or
laziness. He is always engaged in this great
work of saving humanity, and we can only be
in harmony with Him by always being in diligent preparation and accumulation. Those who
are neglectful in preparing for work, will not be
thoughtful in the work. The need of those we
are supposed to help is varied. If we think
and speak in a circle, we will fail to supply the
necessary thought for the Spirit to apply. The
demands of the work are such that anything
less than memories which are entirely consecrated, developed and perfected along evangeli-
cal and practical lines are inadequate.

CONSECRATED INTELLECT.

We are commanded to love God with all the
mind, the same as with all the heart, soul and
strength. God requires that we devote the

rational part of our being fully and entirely to
His service. He requires intelligent worship
and service from His children. His will cannot
be known only through the intellect. That
which is not known cannot be acted upon. The
will of God is to be done in all things. How
can it be if it is not known? He reveals Himself first to the intellect. He cannot be known
as God only through the rational powers. He
may be worshipped as a supreme being through
the intuitions. He is worshipped as a Creator,
Father, Saviour, Friend, when He is known
through the intellect. He reveals Himself
through the intellect to the Spiritual part of
our being, and makes Himself known as a
Father, to be loved and rejoiced in as a loving
parent.

The soul gets to know Him, and the power of
the resurrection of the Lord Jesus being made
conformable to His death. God made the
rational part of our being that we might know
Him as He reveals Himself through it, and
expects and holds us duty bound to consecrate
the whole intellect to Him. We are to think

for Him. There are many things to divert the mind. It is simply impossible until the whole intellect is placed in the current of divine grace. The mind is so prone to wander that unless it is specially and specifically consecrated to God, it is impossible to control it. When it is dedicated to God the sanctifying energy of the Holy Ghost possesses and magnetizes it so fully, that it becomes stable and the thought is kept pure. When it is thus filled with good, holy and heavenly thoughts, purposes and intentions, there is no space for evil thoughts and sur-misings. The mind is active and must be employed; if not, it will seek and find employ-ment, it will engage freely in that which is most congenial to it. When the mind is de-praved it is possessed by low, base, degraded thoughts and cogitations; and when it is re-newed, the thoughts and sentiments are pure, but when it is entirely consecrated it is filled with elevated and heavenly thoughts and visions. The more lofty and elevated the senti-ment, the greater joy there is in it for a conse-crated mind. The conversation being in heaven, the mind will readily soar and enjoy the bliss of the eternal city of God. The degree of purity attained and enjoyed in the mind is consequent upon the consecration to God. God purifies every faculty which is placed at His disposal to operate upon, that which is withheld must remain depraved.

The consecration must be made full and complete, and it must be a constant, living, active devotion to God, kept renewed and vigorous. The purity of the mind will not only be restored, but preserved in a healthy, active, powerful state, fully equipped for all the opposing forces from the world, formality and the devil. Thus it must be with the Christian. " He is consecrated to Christ as a soldier to his flag, as a wife to her husband." The consecrated Christian must be ready to exclaim every moment, " I'm not my own ; I belong to Jesus. I feel, purpose, speak, act, suffer for Him. I have no life but in Him. I am in the world, mingling with men, transacting the business of the world, but I am not of the world. The strong undercurrent of my being flows constantly toward God, and to magnify Jesus, whether by life or by death, is the master-passion of my soul." Consecration must be active and fully carried out in all the details of life. "There is a kind of passive, quiescent, sentimental offering, which some souls seem to make of themselves." Consecration must be such that faith will be the obedient trust of the heart: obedience not hypocritical, but sincere ; not partial, but full; not in starts, but constant ; not slothful, but fervent; not wanting, but perfect. The Christian thus consecrated to God, will have time to read the Word of God and inform his mind, to retire to the closet for strength and the open reward, to attain to all the means of grace and hold fellowship with his brethren in Christ and receive their inspiration, to devote himself to active service for the glory of his Master, to visit the sick and dying, to pray with, talk to, and encourage those who are severely tried and tempted. Consecrated Christians are fearless, they are as bold as lions, they know whom they trust, and are not afraid of being forsaken.

The Master having said, "Fear not, for I have redeemed thee, I have called thee by thy name ; thou art Mine. When thou passest through the waters, I will be with thee ; and through the rivers, they shall not overflow thee ; when thou walkest through the fire, thou shalt not be burned ; neither shall the flame kindle upon thee. For I am the Lord thy God, the Holy One of Israel, thy Saviour. . . . . Since thou wast precious in My sight, thou hast been honorable, and I have loved thee." God's children are to have the mind which was also in Christ Jesus. The command is, " Let this mind be in you." It means a good deal to have the mind of Christ. His mind led Him to deny Himself of everything. Although He was rich, yet "for our sakes He became poor, that we through His poverty might be made rich." He said Himself, that " the foxes have holes, and the birds of the air have nests, but the Son of Man hath not where to lay His head."

And yet He was the eternal Son of God, the only-begotten of the Father, full of grace and truth. All things were made by Him and

through Him, and through Him all things sub-
sist. He denied Himself of all His glory in
heaven and all creature comforts on earth. He
devoted Himself fully to all means that had
been ordained for the salvation of sinners. He
spent whole nights in the mountains alone in
prayer, travelled through the deserts, by the
lake shores, over the mountains, and was
hungry, weary, tired, worn and weak under the
pressure of laborious toil, doing the will of His
Father, rescuing and saving the perishing souls
of men. His mind led Him to bear all manner
of cruel indignities, to suffer reproach, to be
buffeted, to be spat upon, to be despised and
rejected of men, to be a man of sorrows and
acquainted with grief, to be stricken, smitten,
wounded, and bear it all without a murmur or
a complaint. When the children of God have
the mind of Christ, it is the same in them as it
was in Him, there is the same willingness to
bear reproach, to be afflicted, to suffer priva-
tions, to die if need be, to be counted as the off-
scouring of the world, to be cast out as evil, to
spend and be spent for the salvation of souls,

and to glorify God in all things. No cross will
be too heavy, no suffering too great, no work
too hard, in the midst of all opposition, temptation and persecution from ungodly men and
formal Christians, and amidst all the fiery darts
of the wicked one; with cheerfulness and with
joy labor is faithfully prosecuted for Jesus.
"Thou wilt keep him in perfect peace whose
mind is stayed upon Thee." Perfect peace is
consequent upon the mind being stayed upon
God just as much as the heart trusting in Him.
One is impossible without the other. They are
inseparable. When the mind wanders the heart
loses its confidence, and the trust is at once
made weak. "A double-minded man is unstable
in all his ways." Reason is the handmaid of
faith—it helps faith, and gives it an impetus
by which it transcends reason and soars to God.
"Neither be ye of doubtful mind." Doubt is
an act of the mind, just as faith is the trust of
the heart. The latter is largely influenced by
the former. The trust of the heart never can
be full until the mind is fully consecrated,
and all tendencies towards doubt completely

eradicated. The mind must be fully persuaded before the heart can be reached. The truth comes to the mind and persuades it, and reason gives place to faith. Then the mind and heart alike become absorbed in the subject. Each are affected alike and operate in unison. "Let every man be fully persuaded in his own mind." The mind, by nature, in the fallen condition of man is carnal, and is not subject to the law of God, and cannot be until the man is renewed in the spirit of his mind. This carnality is subdued when the soul is regenerated, but it is not completely destroyed until the consecration is complete, and the envies, strifes, etc., are removed by the sanctifying energy of the Holy Ghost. Then God's people are of one mind, "That they all may be one, as Thou Father art in Me and I in Thee." This is what convinces the world and brings sinners to Christ, "that the world may believe that Thou hast sent Me." The mind is to be completely restored, and kept by the peace of God, being stirred up by way of remembrance. "And the peace of God, which passeth all understanding, shall keep

your hearts and minds through Christ Jesus.
Wherefore gird up the loins of your mind, be
sober, and hope to the end for the grace that is
to be brought unto you at the revelation of
Jesus Christ."

CONSECRATED VOICE.

There is no part in the mind, soul or body
which is so difficult to consecrate to God as the
voice. The claim upon it seems to be unyield-
ing, and when the pressure becomes unbearable
it is generally given reluctantly. It is so connected with the unruly member that it is very
difficult to control and consecrate to God. It is a
human creation, but the organs which make the
production and the material out of which it is
made belong to God, therefore the thing formed
is His by absolute right. The consecration of
the voice is an indispensable act of the soul,
which must be perfected before it can truthfully
be said that all is on the altar. There is generally more trouble with the voice than with any
member of the body, any faculty of the mind or
soul. How many there are who are afraid to

hear their own voices in public; if they speak at all it will not be above a whisper, and to hear their own voices in prayer would give them palpitation of the heart and unstring all their nerves. In business transactions, on the public roads, and in the market-places, they can speak in clear, round, fully developed tones, so that they can be heard distinctly across the street. How is it? They have consecrated themselves and their voices to that business. Their hearts are in it and they love to talk about it. They feel perfectly natural in their business and make others who deal with them feel the same freedom. They are at no loss for something to say, and are perfectly indifferent as to how they may express it. They never wait to think about grammar, rhetoric, or finish of expression. They express their feelings and sentiments with a rhetorical flow which is easy and effective. They become eloquent as the occasion demands, when vital interests are at stake. When money is in the question, they can soar to great flights of eloquence and oratory, and carry everything by storm by their impressive and persuasive

style of enforcing and setting home their argu-
ments. You have only to listen to them in
order to be convinced, persuaded, and incited to
action; they would make you take up and
enforce their side of the question. When the
voice is fully and entirely consecrated to God, to
sing His praises, to bear His messages, to call
upon His name, to spread His glory; it will be
a joy to open the mouth and let the abundance
of desire go up in prayer and supplication, to
sing the songs of Zion, making melody in the
heart to the Lord, and speak out from the heart
the Saviour's redemptive glory. The very tones
of the voice will become musical under the
refining fire of the Holy Ghost, and will be
powerful under the Spirit's operations in search-
ing and sounding the lowest depths of the
unbelieving heart. The consecration must be
kept complete, the tongue must be so bridled
and tamed that expression will not be given to
any sentiment that would destroy the influence
or close the mouth from giving expression to
the most sublime and elevated thoughts. The
voice has an internal force, and can have an

unction of divine power which is not readily suppressed or contracted. Such a voice will carry with it a magnetism which will move the most obdurate listener. It is God in the soul modifying the voice and bringing it into touch with the sentiment which gives it expression, and blends spirit with spirit. When the prophetic fire burns in the soul and glows in the countenance, it is carried by the voice, which serves as a bridge to transmit it to an audience. There is a marvellous power in a voice which is fully consecrated and fully possessed by God. Expression can be given to the loftiest sentiment that has ever emanated from a devout soul which has been fired by the baptism of the Holy Ghost. The language will be emphatic and so vibrated by a voice that is clear, full, round and natural with such a tone, as carries with it conviction and persuasion which are irresistible. Voice is a precious gift, to be beautified, developed, consecrated and used for the glory of Him who hath redeemed us. Capable of improvement, adequate for all exigencies, and adapted for the expression of the sublimest thoughts which proceed from the heart inspired by the Holy Ghost.

The powers of articulation and enunciation are given for a specific purpose, and are to be used and not abused. The voice is used, in many cases, to its utmost capacity for the glory of self. Many times it is used for the aggrandizement of some victor of the political or battle-field, and no person is offended because there is some enthusiasm exhibited. When a sinner gets in earnest about salvation, and calls upon God with all his voice, it horrifies some people, and they say that God is not deaf, and their feelings and expressions regarding such praying are bitter and persistent. When the soul is filled with God, it is just as natural for some to be exceedingly boisterous as it is for others to be extremely quiet. Those who are naturally boisterous will suffer much persecution on account of their enthusiasm. Formal Christians and so-called respectable sinners will be agitated, their feelings will be roused, and their denunciations will be emphatic and persistent. The Pharisees as a sect have not all died out yet, and those who do not worship God according to their dictation are disciples that should be rebuked, they are not afraid of the stones crying out. The individual who is naturally quiet, and tries to be boisterous, in order to be like others who make a noise, makes a very grave mistake, and the result of such a course can only prove disastrous to the person and detrimental to the cause of God.

CONSECRATED WILL.

The will stands between God and the soul. " Ye will not come unto Me that ye might have life." The language of the unsaved is, I don't feel like going to-day. The question is, are you willing to give up your sins, your friends, your own way will you surrender ? The stubborn will is not easily subdued. Repentance, faith and conversion are consequent upon the will being so broken that the surrender is complete. How many try to feel better ? they wonder why they cannot have salvation in its richness, power and blessedness, as other people enjoy it. What is the barrier ? The truth is they have never given up their wills, and practically they are rebels, and must continue to be miserable until they give up their wills. They may weep and pray and try to believe, but it is all in vain, the Lord never pardoned a rebel, and He never will. To persuade the will is the work of the preacher. To subdue and completely break it is the work of the Holy Ghost. He does this work as the sinner gives his consent to the truth as it is in Jesus. "A broken and contrite heart, O God, Thou wilt not despise." When the will is thoroughly broken repentance becomes easy. Repentance is the gift of God to the soul that is truly humbled before Him, and faith in Christ has thereby been made possible Some have stubborn wills. They are not easily persuaded (hard to persuade). It is almost impossible to subdue them. You may enlighten the mind, convince the judgment, but the will refuses to submit. Others are not so stubborn. When they receive light, they are ready to be instructed. When their judgments are convinced, they will submit to be directed into the way of life, and they will receive the truth, and

8 e c

be saved by the power of God unto salvation.
None should be discouraged on account of their
stubbornness. All have power to give consent,
and the grace of God wlll thoroughly subdue
when the consent has been given. A strong
will is a great blessing from God to His creature; and when fully subdued, enlightened,
moulded, and developed under the power of
divine grace, it is a power for the glory of God,
and a blessing and comfort to the saint. What
are we unless we have wills of our own? We
would be machines to do the bidding of others.
Our plans, intentions and purposes might be
good, but when we come in contact with others
who thought differently, better or worse, we
would crumble, not having wills of our own.
We can accomplish no great thing for the
Master unless we have wills of our own and
enough of the grace of God to dare to do His
will in all things, at any cost, at any sacrifice or
loss.

It is not enough that the will is subdued and
broken, it must be entirely consecrated to God.
The will must be lost in God's will. "Thy will

be done on earth as it is done in heaven." It is
done perfectly in heaven, so it must be done on
earth in the hearts and and lives of His children, before they are received into heaven. The
question often arises, how can we have a will
and yet have none? There is no contradiction
here. We will to have our wills lost in God's
will, and thus by the continued act of our own
wills we have none; the will is lost in God's
will as the life is hid with Christ in God. It is
difficult for some to consecrate the will, they
like to have their own way in some things.
They would like the Lord to have His way, but
not in all things. God must have His way in
all things small and great. The surrender on
our part must be complete and entire, wanting
in nothing. When it has been made complete
on our part, then the Lord sets us apart to do
His will in the minutest details. The consecrated soul never says no to the Lord. God
helping me, I will, is the language of Canaan.

> "Take my will and make it Thine,
> It shall be no longer mine."

There will be no more "can'ts." The language
of the soul will be, "I can do all things through
Christ which strengtheneth me." The "ifs,"
"can'ts" and "buts" having all passed away

with the entire surrender of the will, the will of
God has become the supreme delight of the soul.

When the soul is entirely consecrated and
each faculty performing its particular function,
the will of God will be a pleasure. Sorrow,
pain and death will have lost their sting, and
the joy of the Lord will be the strength of the
soul. What God wills is best, and the soul
would not wish to have it otherwise. Prosperity and adversity are alike good. The language of the soul having become the very
expression of the Christ, "Not as I will, but as
Thou wilt." His meat was to do the will of
Him that sent Him to finish His work. Work
may at times seem difficult before we reach it,
but when it is undertaken and prosecuted it is
delightful and a source of great blessing. The
experience of the soul will always be clear,
definite and powerful. The full assurance of
understanding having been obtained, the soul
soars and triumphs, knowing that God is working within, to will and to do of His own good
pleasure, the last hindrance having been removed.

> Thy will be done, in Thine own way,
> We will submit, keep Thou, we stray,
> We yield, we work, we sink, we die,
> Thy name be praised, on earth, on high.

PART IV.

PENTECOST.

PENTECOST.

BY

REV. RALPH C. HORNER, B.O.

Author of "Voice Production," etc.

INTRODUCTION

By REV. HUGH JOHNSTON, D.D.

———

TORONTO:

WILLIAM BRIGGS,

WESLEY BUILDINGS.

Montreal: C. W. COATES.   Halifax: S. F. HUESTIS.

INTRODUCTION.

PENTECOST was the second of the three great
annual festivals of the Jews. It concluded
the harvest of the later grains, and as this included
a period of seven complete weeks, it was called the
feast of fifty days, or Pentecost. It was also the
time of the gift of the law, fifty days after the
departure from Egypt.

The Pentecost, then, which marked the day on
which the revelation of the Decalogue took place,
became the grand inauguration day of Christianity.
He who bowed the heavens to throw His voice from
Sinai, now comes in rushing wind and tongue of
flame. That invisible Hand which wrote upon the
tables of stone the ten commandments, now writes
upon the heart the new commandment of love—a
law intensely holy, just and good.

The day of Pentecost was the day of days on
which the Holy Ghost, the Comforter, the divine
guest of the heart, the heavenly Paraclete, proceeding from the Father and the Son, descended in breath

of flame and tongue of fire upon the infant Church. His coming in fulness marks the Christian economy as the dispensation of the Spirit. We live in that holy home upon which He descended more than eighteen hundred and fifty years ago.

His was no passing visit; no sudden but transient illumination; no power fitfully given and suddenly withdrawn. "He dwelleth with you, and shall be in you." The fruits of the Spirit are "love, joy, peace, long-suffering, gentleness, goodness, faith"—all moral excellencies; all manly qualities; all sweet affections. No one can exhaust the alphabet. After the thousands of words, used and unused, the alphabet is capable of making just as many more. So with the graces of Christian character, under the redolent and rich inspiration of the Holy Ghost.

This pentecostal fulness is for all believers—fulness in Christ, in whom dwelleth all the fulness of the Godhead bodily—the baptism of the Spirit, refreshing, renewing, abiding, pouring His own light and love and power through all the life-currents of our being. "Oh, to know the exceeding greatness of His power to usward who believe!"

The purpose of this book is practical. It is to lift believers in thought and feeling and life to higher

levels.   The author's one desire is to awaken in the
hearts of all God's children a supreme longing for
this "pearl of great price."   Certainly, God will not
bestow this gift until we are willing to forego all
other gifts to obtain it.   We are helpless, we are
powerless, we can do nothing without the baptism of
fire.   We must wait for it in the Holy Cœnaculum,
the Upper Room, in obedient faith, and with one
accord plead for it, as hungry children cry for bread.
Oh, that upon every reader of this little volume may
rest the glowing, celestial tongue of fire !   Oh, that
through the truth and through the blood "which
cleanseth from all sin," the Holy Ghost may perform
His purifying work, that so we may receive power,
even that fulness of the Spirit, which qualifies for
abundant labors and abundant successes !

"Awake ! awake ! put on thy strength, O Zion ;
put on thy beautiful garments, O Jerusalem." Shake
thyself from the dust, and put on the power of the
Holy Ghost.   Then shalt thou be a crown of glory
in the hand of the Lord, and a royal diadem in the
hand of our God.

HUGH JOHNSTON.

Toronto, *May*, 1891.

CONTENTS.

THE UPPER ROOM TO-DAY.

" Tarry ye in the city of Jerusalem, until ye be endued with power from on high."

—LUKE xxiv. 49.

PENTECOST.

THE UPPER ROOM TO-DAY.

ONE hundred and twenty people of one heart and one mind in the same place. History refers to no such gathering during the present century, and it is doubtful if the same number could be found in a similar state in all the Christian Church to-day. There are vast numbers who would agree not to attend such a gathering, and many others, who, did they agree on the point of being present, would not be of one heart and mind. The membership of the Christian Church have become so accustomed to doubts and fears, and to a life on a much lower plane, where such a variety of conflicting thoughts and feelings are permitted to hold sway, that they never seriously entertain the thought of meeting the conditions of unity in mind and heart that secure pentecostal blessings. Where shall we go to find one hundred and twenty of one mind and heart? Can that number be found in that state for one day? We think not. However, should such a number be found ready to meet these conditions for one day, can we conclude that they would continue thus for ten days? The limited faith, love, zeal and consecration which we are accustomed to see, justify us in assuming that before ten days had expired many of them would have found an excuse for taking their departure. It does not require much ability to make an excuse. Any ordinary circumstance in life will serve as a basis for shrinking from apostolic devotion. People in general have their homes, friends and business to look after; and when they are worldly-minded they will not be found in the upper room. After being there for eight, nine or ten days, if it were possible to detain them that length of time, would not some of them become impatient, and declare that they had to go home, that their families were in need of their presence and counsel; that some of them might be sick, or they might be dead and buried, having received no intelligence from them since they had left home? We pray thee have us excused. Would they not say that they had their business to look after, that they had to provide for their families; that if they did not provide for their own that they would be denying the faith, and would be worse than infidels. If we do not attend to our own business, other people will not do it for us.

Brethren and sisters, we must go, but pray for us; we want the best that God has for us, pray that we may receive it as we go. We want to enjoy all that there is for us. If they could be induced in any way to tarry in an upper room or seek it at home, it would not be for the purpose of rendering them useful or more efficient in the work of uplifting humanity, but merely that they might be happy. Others might declare, and thus excuse themselves, that they knew of many who were not saved, and if they should die in that state they would certainly be lost forever. Brethren, we cannot stand this, our hearts are burdened for sinners. We must go and tell them about

Jesus. We cannot bear to think of sinners being lost, especially those we have known so well. We must go and preach to them. The harvest truly is great, but the laborers are few. We feel that we are called to preach, and it is woe unto us if we preach not the Gospel. The love we have for souls is more than we can bear. It constrains us. Brethren, we must go. We know that we need this baptism of power that we have been praying for, and pray for us that we may receive it as we go. Will the Lord not bless us as much in preaching to sinners and leading them to Jesus as He will remaining in this upper room, where there are no sinners to be reached? We pray thee have us excused. Others are impatient, and believe they can offer an excuse more plausible than those already offered. They ask for a hearing, and declare that they know many who have not enough to eat, and are almost destitute of clothing to cover their nakedness. They say that they have bread and money, and are ready to spend them in feeding the hungry and clothing the naked. While they are supplying their temporal wants, they believe that they could preach Jesus to them, pray with them, and thus lead them to give up and forsake all for Jesus. These excuses would be very plausible. Most professors of religion would not make any excuse. They would simply absent themselves. They would offer no apology. They never think of seeking the baptism of the Holy Ghost.

Men go out to preach who do not know that it is their privilege to be baptized with the Holy Ghost and with fire. Others go, knowing that they need it, and know it to be their privilege to be anointed for service, but they know also that such a class of preachers are not popular with most congregations in this nineteenth century. They desire and long for the anointing which abideth, but they would much rather be popular. It would not require any effort on our part to believe in the possibility of some one of the number finding fault with his brethren and sisters. We hear so much of it among so-called Christians, that a different state of things would excite surprise and wonder. It seems to be perfectly natural for some to find fault with almost every person that they meet. When Christians get into a grumbling mood, having become soured and stagnant for the want of an outlet, we will be greatly deceived, if we expect from them patience, kindness and long-suffering. Our brethren and sisters would have to be more than human, if we could not find fault with them, were we so disposed.

The Lord Jesus, who was perfect God as well as perfect man, could not please the people. They murmured against Him. They found fault with Him. They called Him a devil. They despised Him. All manner of cruel indignities were heaped upon Him. This was not provoked by men who professed to be openly profane, but by them who essayed to be profoundly religious. The apostles and disciples in the upper room might have found fault with each other if they had been so disposed. They may have been blameless, but they were not faultless. Even if it were possible for them to be faultless, that would not hinder those who were so inclined. Any person in the room might have blamed Thomas for them having to wait so long for the blessing. Thomas had been a doubter, for he had declared that he would not believe except he should see the print of the nails. After having waited for eight or nine days, they could have said that without faith it was impossible to please God. Thomas has been doubting again, and the Lord will not send the blessing unless we all believe. Let us get rid of Thomas, no good can come while we have an Achan in the camp. They might have turned their attention from the Lord, and poor Thomas might have been the victim of all their vituperation. If the forces of all in the upper room had been turned against him, the poor man would have had but little chance for a blessing among them. The room would have been a scene of disunion, disorder and confusion—none blessed, and many excited and irritated. Thomas had the privilege of praying for the baptism of power, and becoming a man of faith, to accomplish wonders for Jesus.

They might have found fault with Peter, if

they had been there for that purpose. Peter was a great man, but had been very weak when severely tried. A maid had caused him to swear that he never knew such a man. The time was not long past. His recreancy was fresh in their minds. If they wished to blame some one of their number for them not being immediately blessed, they could have said, this fellow has been swearing again. Let us hurl him down the stairway. Such a fellow can have no place among us. We have chosen one in the place of Judas, let us cast lots for another, and wash our hands from the blood of this man. Away with such a fellow from our midst. Bless the Lord it was not so in Jerusalem, even it is so now. Peter had the blessed privilege of being among them, and of waiting in prayer for the holy anointing. Bless the Lord, he received it and was the famous preacher of the day—three thousand converted under one sermon and a glorious revival begun. The beloved disciple might have suffered in their midst. They had not forgotten that he wanted to command fire to come down on a certain village of Samaria, because its residents did not receive the Lord. If he had become so irritated with that action of the Samaritans, he is angry now having to wait so long, and God will not bless us while we have this fellow in our circle. They could have found fault with the Saviour Himself, if they wished. He told them that they would be baptized with the Holy Ghost not many days hence. We are here a good many days. A long time to wait for a blessing. We understood that He could have gone up almost in a moment of time, and the Holy Ghost could have come just as quickly. Why keep us here all this time? How much we might have accomplished while we have been here doing nothing? They could have thus murmured, if they had been no better than the Christians of the nineteenth century. They would not tarry one day.

THE
UPPER ROOM IN JERUSALEM.

" *And when the day of Pentecost was fully come,* *they were all with one accord in one place.*"

—Acts ii. 1.

THE UPPER ROOM IN JERU-SALEM.

ONE hundred and twenty tarrying for ten days in an upper room in Jerusalem, praying, praising blessing God and waiting for power. They had been told by the Master to tarry in the city of Jerusalem, until they would be endued with power from on high. These men and women were not like most Christians of this century. They would not attempt to justify themselves in breaking the commands of God. The Saviour had said to them, if ye love Me keep My commandments. He had said also, if a man love Me, he will keep My words. These Christians were conscious that their salvation depended upon their obedience. They had taken it to heart, and were going to obey or die in the attempt. They had learned that to obey was better than to sacrifice. Obedience had become natural. They did not obey Him through fear, but through love. They were there not to break the commands of God, but to keep them. Their allegiance to Christ was not flattery, it was true, not like most Christians of the nineteenth century. They did not suppose that they could break the commands of God in thought, word and deed, and still be justified in the sight of God without intermission. They were told to wait for power. They felt their need of this anointing. They did not expect to receive it by ignoring the command of the Saviour, but by strictly observing it. There was a very marked difference between them and the Christians of this century. They were consecrated and willing to do His will, for the glory of His name, and the salvation of souls. Christians of this century, as a rule, have an extremely low conception of what consecration means.

The Christians in the upper room in Jerusalem were seeking for power to work, to endure, and to rescue the perishing. Most Christians of the present time seek for happiness; not for power—for a joyful experience; not the will of God—for a general good time; not the glory of the Master—for an experience that will secure to them perfect ease; not suffering or hard toil for the cause of the Redeemer. The apostles were willing to obey at any cost, peril or loss. The Christians of this century will obey if it secures to them ease and wealth. They endured hardness as good soldiers of Jesus Christ; Christians now seek for happiness and the good-will of men. The Saviour had said, ye shall be baptized with the Holy Ghost not many days hence. And also, ye shall receive power after that the Holy Ghost is come upon you; and ye shall be witnesses unto Me both in Jerusalem, and in all Judea, and in Samaria, and unto the uttermost part of the earth. They were one in believing the Saviour's promises. They had no reason to doubt, but good reason to believe. The Saviour had said many things, and all had come to pass; every promise He had made during the three years of His teaching was fulfilled. He had told them that He would suffer many things, that He would be rejected, that He would die, be buried and rise again the third day. These things had all come to pass.

The faithfulness of Christ to fulfil His promises, and the expectant spirit of His disciples on this occasion, are beautifully and forcibly illustrated by a story concerning a little boy and his faithful mother. All mothers are not faithful. Many mothers tell lies very frequently. They promise to punish their children, and they do not do it. They promise to give them certain things at appointed seasons, and they fail to do so. They say to their children, you must not do this or that, and they stand and look at them doing the very things that they forbid them to do. They fail to keep their promises in these things, and when their children cannot believe them in these instances, they cannot believe them in others. This boy's mother was not like that. Whatever she promised, whether it was a punishment or a pleasure, it was forthcoming without fail. She called him to her bedside when dying, and told him that she was going to die, but that God would come and take care of him. When she was dead and buried, the boy commenced to think over what his mother had said. He con-

cluded that God would surely come, for, said
he, my mother said He would. She always told
me the truth. He commenced to look for God
to come. He was outside the house looking in
every direction for God to come to him. A man
came along, and asked him what he was looking
for; and he told him the story of his mother,
and what she had said when dying. The boy
said, with much assurance, " God will come, for
mother said He would." The man replied, " God
sent me to take care of you, and you are to
come to my home." The boy immediately
accepted, and started to his new home.

The disciples had a Master and a most faithful one, and when leaving them, He said that
God would come and take care of them. "If I
go not away, the Comforter will not come unto
you; but if I depart, I will send Him unto
you." They had the Saviour's promise and they
all believed it. They were all of one accord on
this very vital point. They not only obeyed
the command, but they believed the promise.
They were agreed to pray for the blessing until
they received it.

" These all continued with one accord in prayer and supplication." They did not pray as many do at the present time. It has never been a very difficult matter to get men to commence to pray. The trouble always arises when they are urged to pray until they get what they need. The Jacob-like spirit is not found among the people of God now. The disciples had it. The Bible tells us so. They "continued" in prayer and supplication. They sought the anointing that Jesus had promised. They did not pray all around the world, the community, or the congregation. How many pray, Lord, we need it, give it to us? They do not pray for themselves, but for some brother or sister that they think needs it very much. How few cry out in agony of soul for themselves? I need it, send it to me! O Lord, I cannot do without it. The hundred and twenty pleaded their individual cases. I need it. Baptize my soul with the Holy Ghost and with fire. Oh, let it come upon me. Jesus, I plead the promise. I cannot let go. Oh, let it come upon me now. I will not let Thee go. I cannot yield. I am weak. God help me. I shall never leave this place until I receive the promise. Dear Jesus, now baptize me with fire. My soul is yearning. Come, oh, come, Lord Jesus! I cannot wait. Bless me, even me, O my father! Let the Holy Ghost come upon me now. I have no power to work. I am helpless. Souls are perishing. I have not been able to reach them in the past. Oh, for power to sound the depths of the unbelieving heart! Oh, for power; send it now, just now! Amen! Let it come upon my soul. Yes, it is coming! Glory! Glory! Hallelujah!

The disciples did not expect to receive it without praying for it. They had been learning of Jesus. They had heard Him pray. They had seen Him go away alone to plead with the Father for the anointing. They understood that when He got into an agony He prayed more earnestly. They had learned that they were to ask in His name for such blessings as they needed. He had told them that if they would ask anything in His name, that He would do it. " If ye abide in Me, and My words abide in you, ye shall ask what ye will, and it shall be done unto you." They understood that they had to seek definitely for what they needed. The Saviour had said, "Ask, and it shall be given you ; seek, and ye shall find ; knock, and it shall be opened unto you."

The disciples were never seen going around whining for a blessing. When they felt their need, they went to God in prayer, and they always received just what they sought. They were never weak and unfitted for their work ; God supplied all their need out of His riches in glory by Christ Jesus. The followers of Christ in this age do not expect to have all their needs supplied. There are many weaklings in our day. They never seek for power to do something glorious for Jesus. How few speak of the baptism of the Holy Ghost and fire. It is not in the prayers of professing Christians, and consequently cannot be found in their lives or testimonies. It is not preached from the pulpits, and we could not expect to hear it from the pews. The Lord anoint the ministry, so that it may be preached. This is the power of

the Gospel, which is to bring the world to Jesus.
The Lord inspire our prayers. The Lord reveal
it from His Word to His children, as their privilege, so that it may be sought, found, and the
world made to feel it. Mighty God, move us.
Blessed Saviour, plead for us. Holy Ghost,
create the hungering and thirsting; let us
keenly feel our need of the anointing. Indite
and inspire us to pray for it. Increase our
faith. Father, for the sake of Thy Son, baptize
us with the Holy Ghost and fire. The disciples
believed that Jesus would do what He had
promised. The Holy Ghost would certainly
come, for Jesus had said that He would send the
Comforter. He had told them that they would
receive power after that the Holy Ghost had
come upon them. The baptism of the Holy
Ghost was the seal to His ministry. John the
Baptist had said that He would baptize with
the Holy Ghost and with fire. They were
assured by Jesus that they would receive the
blessing not many days hence.

The disciples were men of faith; three years
previous to this occasion they determined that

they would believe. They had exercised faith
in Jesus many times, and according to their
faith it had always been done unto them.
Their faith had been confirmed by the resurrection of the Saviour, and much more abundantly
by His appearing among them ten times. They
had received the full assurance of faith, hope
and understanding. The Saviour had opened
up their understanding, that they might understand the Scriptures. He had breathed upon
them, and said, Receive ye the Holy Ghost.
They had a blessed experience, and were strong
in faith. They had returned to Jerusalem with
great joy, and were continually in the temple
praising and blessing God. Their faith had
risen to an active, jubilant state, as well as a
state of perfect obedience to the will of God.
They were not hoping that they would receive
the blessing that they were commanded to
wait for. They believed in their hearts that
they would receive this blessing they so much
needed for the work, and that was promised by
the Saviour. Their faith was definite, active
and present. It brought the power. They all

had faith. None had to wait until the next day. They were all filled with the Holy Ghost, and wisdom, and power. They believed in the vigorous exercise of what faith they had, and that made it possible for them to receive more. They never dishonored or offended God by asking for more faith without using to its utmost capacity what they had already received. They had good reason to believe the promise of God could not fail them. Their faith took hold of the truth, and the Holy Ghost came down and sat upon each of them. They were all filled with the Holy Ghost. Not some, but one hundred and twenty. Not the twelve apostles, but all in the upper room.

Not some believing that it was for them, and others trying to help them, but each individual pressing his own case, until the baptism was received. Their faith took hold of the promise, and did not waver until the power of the truth was realized by the anointing which abideth. They felt that they needed the baptism. They had been using what power they had, and had become conscious of their need of the special baptism of power. They had enjoyed and used the grace which had been given to them, and were hungering and thirsting for more. They had learned by their efforts that there was work to be done which never would be accomplished by them unless they should receive this special blessing promised by the Saviour. The Saviour had told them that they would do the works that He did, and also that they would do greater things, because He was going to the Father. They knew that unless they should receive something more than they had received up to that time, that they could not accomplish what Jesus did. And they were to do greater things. They were to go and preach to the very men who had crucified their Lord and Master. They felt their need of power to charge home the death of the Lord Jesus on His murderers in such a way that they would be pricked in their heart, and be led to repentance toward God and faith in the Lord Jesus.

They needed power to get three thousand converted in one day as a preparation for the great revival that was to follow. They felt that they could not shake the unbelieving heart unless God would give them a special baptism, and He having promised it, they were one in seeking for it until they had received it. Their Lord and Master had been crucified by the men that they were going to preach to, and their own lives were in peril; they were required to be in readiness to lay down their lives for the cause of Christ. A little maid had caused the boldest one of their number to swear that he never knew such a man. When baptized by the Holy Ghost he could charge home the death of the Saviour on His murderers, and thousands were led to the Saviour under his sermon on the day of pentecost. When these men prayed after they were baptized, the place where they were assembled together shook, prison doors flew open, fetters immediately fell off, their feet were freed from the stocks, and angels conducted them out of their cells. They were a terror to all their enemies, and a praise to them that were good.

THE TESTING TIME.

If the disciples had been like the Christians of the present day, they would have wanted to know what He meant by this: ye shall receive power after that the Holy Ghost is come upon you. They could have declared that they had power. They might have said that when they were converted they had received the Holy Ghost. They were converted under the preaching of the Lord Jesus. They had heard Him say many times go in peace and sin no more. They had been sitting for three years under the preaching of Him who spake as never man spake. They could have claimed a very high standard of Christian experience, after having listened so often to the teachings of Him who was perfect God, as well as perfect man. His words were full of the Spirit, and they were the power of God to every one that believed them. They could have quoted the Lord's own words: Now ye are clean through the word which I have spoken unto you. They could have reasoned as follows: Those who are clean

have power with God, for it is only sin that
makes the children of God weak; we are clean,
therefore we have power. They could Have
claimed more than conversion, for undoubtedly
they had received more. John Wesley said
that when he was converted his heart was
strangely warmed; but while Jesus talked with
His disciples by the way their hearts burned
within them. The Saviour had prayed for
their sanctification, and His prayer must have
been answered. They could have referred to
the evidences that they had that this work was
accomplished in them, if any more than faith
had been necessary. The Lord Jesus did more
than pray for them, He breathed upon them
and said, Receive ye the Holy Ghost. They
could have said that they were ordained to
preach; that they had received power to heal
the sick, to cleanse the lepers, to raise the
dead, to cast out devils, to work all kinds of
miracles, and that the devils were subject to
them. If there ever were a Christian people
in the history of the Church of God who could
have claimed to have power, these disciples had

the strongest grounds for doing so. They were not the kind of Christians that claim to have all when they only possess a part of what God has for them. They were thankful for what they had received, but were not satisfied with anything less than God had promised them for a qualification for work.

TESTIMONY OF JOHN THE BAPTIST.

" *The same is He which baptizeth with the Holy Ghost.*"

—John i. 33.

TESTIMONY OF JOHN THE BAPTIST.

He confessed that he was not the Christ, but was only a voice. He was a voice that was heard. He was not afraid to speak. He delivered the message that God gave him. He was a plain preacher, and charged home the sins of the people upon them. O generation of vipers! was hurled at those who came to his baptism—bring forth fruits meet for repentance. He defined very clearly and specifically what Jesus came to do for a lost race. His teaching was not mystified. He taught definitely what he wanted the people to know. He explained to his disciples the nature of his work, and directed their attention more fully to the work of Jesus. He was to decrease, and the Lord Jesus was to increase. John the Baptist told of two very important things that Jesus came to do. The first was that He should take away the sin of the world. When he was turning the attention of his disciples from himself to Jesus, he pointed Him out as the Saviour who would save from all sin. This was the point of attraction for them, He was to take away their sins. "Behold the Lamb of God, which taketh away the sin of the world." John did not know Him, but God had revealed unto him that upon whom he should see the Spirit descending and remaining, the same should baptize with the Holy Ghost. John bare record, saying that he saw the Spirit descending from heaven like a dove, and remaining upon Him. "The same is He which baptizeth with the Holy Ghost."

Jesus came to take away the guilt of sin by His justifying grace. "Be it known unto you, therefore, men and brethren, that through this man is preached unto you the forgiveness of sins; and by Him all that believe are justified from all things." He came to take away the condemnation and power of sin. "There is, therefore, now no condemnation to them which are in Christ Jesus." "He that believeth is not condemned." He came to take away the pollu-

tion of sin by the cleansing efficacy and energy
of His precious blood applied to the conscience,
purging it from sin and dead works to serve the
living God. His name was called Jesus, "for He
shall save His people from their sins." "If we
confess our sins, He is faithful and just to forgive us our sins, and to cleanse us from all
unrighteousness." "If we walk in the light, as
He is in the light, we have fellowship one with
another, and the blood of Jesus Christ His Son
cleanseth us from all sin." Jesus did not come
to save the world from all sin, but His own
people. He can save them and keep them
every whit whole. Those who are not being
saved and kept are not His. They either were
not converted or they are backsliders. How
few of those who profess to be the faithful
followers of the Lord Jesus expect to be saved
from all sin. Many of them profess to be trying
to keep what religion they have, and are trying
to deepen the work of grace. They do not want
to be saved from all sin ; they could not keep
themselves in that state. The probabilities are
that they had no religion, and it is very possible
that they never had any.

The children of God do not sin. " Whosoever is born of God doth not commit sin ; for His seed remaineth in him." "Whosoever abideth in Him sinneth not." They are kept by the power of God through faith. What they have received keeps them, and it is a power in them which enables them to ask and believe for all they need. When they repent of inbred sin and believe in Jesus for salvation from the being of sin, their troubles about themselves are ended, and their whole strength and energy will be spent in helping others.

When they are baptized with the Holy Ghost and fire, it is easy for them to work and win for Jesus. How few profess to be baptized with the Holy Ghost and with fire. Not one out of every thousand who call themselves the followers of the Lord Jesus. Not one out of every hundred expect or even hope to have such an experience. Most Christians do not know that there is such an experience for them to attain unto ; and if they did know they would not trouble themselves to seek after it, lest they should be expected to do something for Jesus.

They are at ease in Zion. They never did any-thing for Jesus, and they do not expect to ever put forth an effort to win a soul for Jesus. Holiness preaching is distasteful to them. The baptism of power is perfectly disgusting to them. If God would send a pentecost to many congregations who call themselves evan-gelical, they would be terrified beyond descrip-tion. Should one half of the congregation receive the anointing, the other half would be perfectly horrified at them. Many of them would run out of the place of worship not to return. Others would return to their homes, murmuring, scolding, finding fault, not in the spirit of Christ, but seemingly possessed.

THE CHRIST ANOINTED.

" *The Spirit of God descending like a dove* . . .
upon Him."

—MATTHEW iii. 16.

THE CHRIST ANOINTED.

"GOD anointed Jesus of Nazareth with the Holy Ghost and with power." These questions come up: Why was Jesus baptized with the Holy Ghost and with power, when He had no sin to be purged away? Why was it necessary for Him to be baptized with the Holy Ghost? Was He not perfect God as well as perfect man? The baptism of the Holy Ghost was not designed by God to save His people from their sins. The soul must be fully saved from inbred, as well as actual sins, before it is anointed for service. Jesus, having no sin to be saved from, was fully prepared for the anointing of the Holy Ghost. The Holy Ghost came and abode upon Him. He was anointed with the Holy Ghost, and not with wisdom or fire, but with power. The Holy Ghost came upon Him from heaven like a dove. Jesus had no sin, either actual or inbred, and the Holy Ghost came upon Him in this dove-like appearance,

indicating His immaculate purity and impecca-
bility. He came upon the apostles like fire,
indicating their need of continual purging, on
account of their sins of ignorance, infirmities,
etc. This anointing is always followed by
something remarkable. Jesus was led into the
wilderness by the Spirit to fast for forty days,
and then to be tempted of the devil. He
needed this anointing for such a trial. It gave
Him power to endure. He did not live by
bread alone. Neither did He yield to temptation. No doubt He was severely tried when
tempted by the devil, after having fasted so
long. He was made perfect through suffering,
and He knows how to succor those who are
tempted. He did not remain satisfied with one
anointing of the Spirit. He was strengthened
different times when working out the great
redemption. He was more than baptized with
the Holy Ghost. He was also baptized, not
with faith, not with love, not with wisdom, but
with power. Power to suffer, power to endure,
power to conquer, and He finished the work ;
and then all power in heaven and in earth was

given to Him. He had a human body and soul
to be operated upon. He had human affections
which were energized by the Holy Ghost. He
had a body, which was pregnated by the power
of God, and so permeated, that it became
strengthened for the purpose of suffering, and
accomplishing the work that He came to do.

Jesus was not baptized with this baptism to
make Him wise, shrewd, humble, faithful, true,
devoted or kind. He was the perfect embodiment of all these, and knew all things, past,
present and future. It gave Him nothing new,
only power to use what he had in possession.
If it was absolutely necessary for Jesus to be
baptized with the Holy Ghost, how much more
His frail creatures, with their fallibility, infirmities, ignorances, etc. He had more than a
perfect human nature; He had a perfect divine
nature in the same body. We are to be like
Him, and how can we except we receive the
same manifestations of power in our souls and
bodies? We, with all our imperfections, and
the blessed Christ with all His perfections, can
we be like Him unless we be baptized with the

4

same Spirit ? The record of John the Baptist was, that upon whom he should see the Spirit descending and remaining upon Him, the same is He which baptizeth with the Holy Ghost. The Bible teaches us that those who have the hope of seeing Christ and being like Him, purify themselves even as He (Christ) is pure. How is this experience to be attained, if not by the baptism of the Holy Ghost and fire ? Is it not the refining fire that goes through the heart, that purifies as silver, and refines as Gold ? The Scriptures teach us that he that doeth righteousness is righteous, even as He is righteous. How can this state of being right with God be attained only by the blessed baptism of power. We are commanded to have the mind in us which was also in Christ Jesus ; the mind must be stamped upon and implanted in us by the baptism of the Holy Ghost. As He is so are we in this world, not equal in knowledge, judgment, etc., but perfectly cleansed from all evil tendencies and propensities, and baptized with the same baptism of the Holy Ghost. Having received the same baptism of power, all the members of our bodies, and every faculty of our souls, perform their particular functions according to our capability; just as fully as His do according to His omnipotence. Come, great Spirit, with all thy mighty power; come, and anoint us thy people; come, and abide with us; come, and guide us into all truth ; come, and make us like the blessed Jesus. Come, oh, come, come now.

THE EXPERIENCE OF THE APOSTLES.

"And they were all filled with the Holy Ghost."

—ACTS ii. 4.

THE EXPERIENCE OF THE APOSTLES.

JESUS has not left on record the words that He used when assuring the apostles that their sins were forgiven them, as He has done regarding other sinners who came unto Him. To some He said, "Thy sins be forgiven thee;" to others He said, "Go in peace and sin no more;" and to others, "According to your faith be it unto you." Many people would have seemingly been better satisfied in their minds, if He had left on record what He had said to His disciples on this point. It might have saved them from grave errors, but we are inclined to think that it would have made no difference. The Lord Jesus did better than tell us the exact words that He used when forgiving the sins of these men. He has told us their definite experiences after three years of service on probation in the kingdom of God. He has given us to know that they were not only saved by His grace, but were kept by the power of God, through faith unto salvation. Sometimes it does not mean much for sinners to know their sins forgiven, as in the case of the nine lepers. In this case it meant a good deal, only one out of twelve was lost. "Those that Thou gavest Me I have kept, and none of them is lost, but the son of perdition." He has given us their experiences in very clear, definite language, so that we need not make any mistake, or be in the dark on this question of vital importance.

In the Gospel of John xiii. chapter and 10th verse, we read: "Jesus saith to him, He that is washed needeth not save to wash his feet, but is clean every whit; and ye are clean, but not all." He has declared here that eleven of them were every whit clean, and needeth not to wash save their feet. Stronger language to express how fully their sins were forgiven them, could not be used. He has not only pronounced them clean, but every whit clean. There is a very broad sense in which those who have been regenerated may be said to be clean. These men had not only received the grace of God, but that grace had so fully kept them that the Saviour could pronounce them clean without any limitation.

In the gospel of John xv. chapter and 3rd verse He said also, " Now ye are clean through the word which I have spoken unto you." In this testimony He has declared that they were clean, and also the means by which they had attained unto this experience. This experience was not a natural attainment, it was not attained unto by good works, neither did they grow into it, but as Jesus said, " through the word which I have spoken unto you." The language used in both of these testimonies is not only definite, clear and explicit, but very strong, and fully expresses the state of a soul that has been justified from all things. These portions of Scripture are so strong that they are used by some modern teachers of holiness to express the state and experience of certain persons who are said to be entirely sanctified. It is a fact which is indisputable that they fully express the experience of every soul newly born into the kingdom of our Lord Jesus.

In this same gospel (xvii. 9-16), he has more
fully set forth their experience. He has given
us the relation that they held to the Father.
He declared, "They are Thine," "And all Mine
are Thine, and Thine are Mine; and I am glorified in them." The Lord Jesus was glorified in
the experience of these men. He prayed to the
Father to keep through His own name those
that the Father had given to Him, affirming
that while He was with them that He had kept
them. In verse 14 He expressed the separation
that had been maintained between His disciples
and the world. He said that the world hated
them because they were not of the world, even
as He was not of the world. This He has
repeated in verse 16, showing and emphasizing
that these men were not of the world, that they
had been more than converted, that they had
retained their religious experience by separating
themselves from the ungodly, and had consecrated themselves to God. This consecration
had been kept renewed for three years, so that
Jesus could say of them, they are not of the
world, even as I am not of the world. This

language is strong, but it is the testimony of Jesus concerning the experience of His disciples, who had followed Him for three years. The testimony of any man who had been with them for that length of time should be accepted, provided he were a Christian. Jesus knew all things. He made no mistakes.

Jesus had used very strong language describing their definite experiences after three years of probation in the service and work of their Master. And yet He knew that they had inbred sin in them, and was very forcibly impressed with their extreme weakness in the hour of trial. He knew how hard it was for Thomas to keep from doubting, that it was perfectly natural for him to say, I will not believe, that when temptation or provocation would be severe he would yield. He was fully cognizant of the weakness and fearfulness of Peter, that, although seemingly bold, and confident that even all men would deny Him that *he* would not, that a little maid would completely demoralize him in the hour of darkness; that the very time that Peter should be strong and of a good courage, he would deny Him altogether, and that wickedly by swearing that he did not know such a man. Even John, the beloved disciple, was irritable, and wanted to call down fire from heaven on a certain village of Samaritans because they did not receive Jesus as he thought they should have done. He did not leave His disciples in this state. He was desirous that they should have a better experience, and He prayed for them : " Sanctify them through Thy truth, Thy word is truth." (John xvii. 17.) He prayed for their entire sanctification. Sanctified through the truth or truly sanctified. Saved from anger, pride, fear, selfishness, doubt, envy, jealousy, etc. ; that they might have similar experiences. In this intercessory prayer He asked five times that they might become one, that the world might believe that the Father had sent Him. He also asked that the glory which the Father had given Him might be given unto them, that the world might more than believe, that the world might know that the Father had sent Him, and had loved them as He loved His Son Jesus Christ, the

world's Redeemer. They were to be one in the
fullest sense, to be perfect in one.   This oneness
was to be the same as that which existed
between the Father and the Son. "That they
all may be one, as Thou the Father art in Me
and I in Thee." "I in them and Thou in Me."
This was to be a perfection and completeness
without any conscious or visible want. It was
God's way of making the world believe and
know that He was the very Christ, the Saviour
of the world.

It has been said that true prayer is always
answered. Prayer offered according to the will
of God, indited and inspired by God the Holy
Ghost, through God the Son, to God the Father,
could not possibly remain unanswered. Jesus
prayed under the power of the Holy Ghost. We
could not suppose that there was any lack in
His prayer. Everything that He did was perfect. He spake, and it was done. Should we
conclude, then, that the apostles were sanctified
because Jesus prayed to the Father to sanctify
them, seeing that His prayer must of necessity
be answered ? If we should come to such a

conclusion, we would be perfectly safe, and be beyond the reach of critics, in any attacks they might feel disposed to make. We are not forced into such a conclusion. The Scriptures teach us plainly, that after His resurrection, Jesus led His disciples into the experience that He had prayed that they might receive. The words used by the Master are on record to help our faith and understanding. After the blessed Christ rose from the tomb, He met His disciples ten times, He blessed them, confirmed, perpetuated, and perfected their faith before He ascended. John Wesley said, that when he was converted that he felt his heart strangely warmed in him ; but when Jesus conversed with His disciples on the way to Emmaus, they felt more than strangely warmed, their hearts burned within them.

When the disciples were assembled together for fear of the Jews, Jesus appeared in their midst, and said, "Peace be unto you." (John xx. 19, 28.) He spake to their fearful hearts, and fear gave place to peace and joy, then the disciples were glad when they saw the

Lord. Then He spake again and said, " Peace
be unto you," and gave them their commission,
as the Father had sent Him, even so said He, " I
send you." Then He breathed upon them, and
said unto them, " Receive ye the Holy Ghost."
Thomas was not present, and when the other
disciples told him that they had seen the Lord,
he declared that he would not believe, unless he
would see the print of the nails, and thrust his
hand into the open side. Eight days after, when
Thomas was present, Jesus appeared in their
midst again, and said, " Peace be unto you."
When Thomas was asked by the Christ, to put
his fingers into the prints of the nails, and
thrust his hand into His side, and be not faith-
less but believing, he cried out, " My Lord and
my God." Thomas was immediately saved
from that inbred sin. Where there is no doubt
there can be no sin. The fulness of faith will
immediately bring full salvation.

These were not the only times that Jesus
appeared unto His disciples. In these portions
of Scripture He spoke three times unto them,
and said, " Peace be unto you." If we were

confined to these portions of Scripture for establishing the fact that they had received the blessing that Jesus prayed that they might receive, we would not be at any loss. When Jesus said, " Peace be unto you," He said it with authority and power, not as a mere man, but as the God-man, perfect man and perfect God. He did more than give them peace. He breathed upon them, and said, " Receive ye the Holy Ghost." The Lord Jesus did not meet with, and talk to, and breathe upon them in a formal way without producing some effect. He spake as never man spake. When He spake, immediately sins were forgiven, lepers were cleansed, devils were cast out, and the dead were raised. None were obliged to wait, and there were no failures. When He breathed upon them, He commanded them to receive the Holy Ghost. Any misgivings that may have been troubling them about His resurrection were all removed from them when they handled Him and knew that He had flesh and bones. He ate with them, and destroyed any lingering doubts in their minds regarding the mystery of His being raised from the dead. He opened up their understanding, so that they could understand what Moses and the prophets had written, and what was in the Psalms concerning Him. These men were not ignorantly sanctified. Their minds were opened up, so that they could do more than enjoy the good things of the kingdom. They could teach them to others. They were parting with their blessed Master, but they were not sorrowful, although He was all and in all to them. They worshipped Him, and their souls were ecstatic. They returned to Jerusalem, not in heaviness, not in mourning, not in gloom, not downcast, but with great joy. Before they received this blessing, when He spake of parting with them sorrow filled their hearts. " But because I have said these things unto you, sorrow hath filled your hearts." The entire sanctification of their nature prevented them from feeling the arrow of separation, and prepared them to obey His command and return to Jerusalem to await the anointing which abideth. They returned with great joy.

We are not obliged to establish the fact, that

5

the disciples were sanctified before the day of
Pentecost, on any Scriptures that we have
quoted. We have the Saviour's infallible testimony to the fact that they had received it.
The visible effect that was to be produced upon
them was that they should be one, as the Father
and the Son were one. This the Christ asked
for five times in His intercessory prayer. The
Lord Jesus is the witness; He has declared that
this definite experience had been attained unto
by them. In His word we read it so: "These
all continued with one accord in prayer and
supplication." (Acts i. 14.) They had attained
the very experience that Jesus prayed that they
might receive. They were all of one accord.
He prayed that they all might be one. We
could conceive that it would be possible
for Christians to reach a point where spirit
would blend with spirit, without being entirely
sanctified. They did more than touch a point,
they had an experience of that kind, and continued in that state. These all *continued* with
one accord—there was nothing spasmodic about
it, they remained in that state of unity before
God.

This was not an experience of a moment, of a day, of a week, but until the day of Pentecost had fully come. They continued in that state of oneness for ten days. The Scriptures teach us that they continued in that state of oneness from the time that they entered Jerusalem until the day of Pentecost. "And when the day of Pentecost was fully come, they were all with one accord in one place." (Acts ii. 1.) The work was radical. It reached every part of their beings. It was not wanting in any respect. It bound them together, as the Father and the Son. It kept them of one accord that length of time. The grace that saves for a moment will keep for ten days, and that which would make them one, as the Father and the Son are one, for ten days, would enable them to have grace to remain in that state the rest of their lives. Then they could serve God without fear in holiness and righteousness before Him all the days of their lives. In such a state of perfected salvation, their faith would increase, their hopes would be confirmed, and their love kept perfect. Their souls would be fully prepared for the baptism of the Holy Ghost. There would be no conscious effort to receive that anointing. It would be received by faith without a struggle, and it would permeate every faculty of the soul and every member of the body. Jesus did not part with His disciples until they were fully saved, and were rejoicing in all the fulness of the glorious redemption. They returned to Jerusalem with great joy. They were told to tarry in Jerusalem until they would be endued with power from on high. Jesus had assured them that He would send upon them the promise of the Father. They had the Saviour's promise to rest upon while they remained in the upper room for the anointing.

There are some teachers who say that the disciples did not receive the blessing of entire sanctification until the day of Pentecost. No great writer on this subject has made such a statement. Others have said that the disciples were not converted until the day of Pentecost. They affirm that they were only seekers of salvation, that they did not receive the adoption of sons until that day. Such teaching is preposterous. It is to say that Jesus forgave other sinners, but did not forgive His own disciples. He had told others to go in peace and sin no more, and let the chosen apostles go around in their sins, trying to bring others into the light, and they in darkness themselves. It is to charge home on the Lord Jesus the crime of having sent them to preach, heal the sick, cast out devils, etc., and they not saved themselves. The Bible saves us from the necessity of making such palpable errors. It is also an error to affirm that they did not receive the blessing of entire sanctification until the day of Pentecost.

The Bible teaching on all these essential points is clear and explicit. They were not told to remain there to repent, to increase their faith, to complete their consecration, to seek for cleansing; but simply to remain until they would be endued with power from on high. John Wesley taught that the repentance that precedes entire sanctification is deeper than that which precedes regeneration. There is nothing to lead us to infer that the disciples were repenting for ten days in the upper room.

They were there in prayer, in supplication, in praise, in blessing, and they continued in that state until they were baptized with power. "And He led them out as far as to Bethany, and He lifted up His hands, and blessed them. And it came to pass, while He blessed them, He was parted from them and carried up into heaven. And they worshipped Him, and returned to Jerusalem with great joy; and were continually in the temple praising and blessing God."

The apostles and disciples remained in Jerusalem, and were in the upper room when the time had come, and they were baptized with the Holy Ghost and fire. They were all baptized. There were no exceptions. None of them had to wait until the next day. When the fulness of the time for the new dispensation had come, they all received the power of the Holy Ghost. The Christians in apostolic times never expected to, and never had to wait for a blessing. Holy people never have to wait or agonize before God for a blessing. When they become fully conscious of their need, they have nothing to do but ask and receive all that their souls desire. These .disciples of the Lord Jesus had been working in the vineyard of the Lord, and had become fully conscious that they had great need of power, in order to be efficient workers for Jesus. They had been told by the Lord Jesus that they should receive power after that the Holy Ghost had come upon them. They did not expect to have power before the Holy Ghost had come upon them, for Jesus had said it would be after. They had learned to obey the Lord Jesus in all things, both great and small, and He had commanded them to tarry in Jerusalem until they would be endued with power from on high. They had received power to believe every word which the Master had spoken. Entire sanctification could not possibly do anything less than that for them.

Entire sanctification can be nothing less than the fulness of faith, and it is positively a good deal more. The fulness of faith will immediately bring the fulness of the blessing of the Gospel included in the covenant of grace. The apostles received the anointing the moment the fulness of the dispensation of the Holy Ghost had come. There is no limit to the power of the anointing of the Holy Ghost, in this His dispensation, and this power will be received by the children of God according to their faith. The faith of those who have been fully anointed once knows no limit. God has given all things to His children. "All things are yours, . . . ye are Christ's." All things are possible to him that believeth. The apostles were believers in the fullest sense of the word, and they claimed the baptism of the Holy Ghost, in all its richness and power, for actual service for the glory of the Lord Jesus. While they were praying and believing, suddenly there came a sound from heaven, as of a rushing mighty wind, and there sat upon each of them tongues of fire, and they were all filled with the Holy Ghost. This was not a reception of the Holy Ghost, they had received Him when their sins were forgiven, and a fuller manifestation of His presence, when Jesus breathed upon them and said, Receive ye the Holy Ghost. This was the reception of the gift of the Holy Ghost. They were baptized with power to accomplish wonders, in the name, and for the glory of Jesus. They had been working for Jesus, but had accomplished very little, compared with what they did after they had received this anointing for service. Jesus had said, "The works that I do shall he do also; and greater works than these shall he do; because I go unto my Father." He that believeth was to do these greater things. The disciples did the same works, and they did greater things. The Lord Jesus did not see three thousand converted in one day under His preaching. The immediate result of the Pentecost was the conversion of three thousand in one day and the beginning of a glorious revival.

When the Lord Jesus ascended, He sent forth the Holy Ghost upon His disciples, He baptized them with the Holy Ghost. Under the Holy Ghost they accomplished the greater things. These men had power to shake the gates of hell, to sound the depths of the unbelieving heart, to open up the gates of heaven, to bring heaven down into their midst, when they prayed by their faith. They were men of marvellous power; God was with them in all they undertook to do for Him, and their efforts were crowned with marvellous success. They could suffer the lash, the prison, the cell, the chains, the stocks, and they could do these things with joy. They could and did preach in defiance of the law of the Sanhedrim, the priests, the prison, the cell, the chains and stocks. When they prayed the very building in which they were assembled shook. ' They could pray prison doors open, and cause the place to tremble until the fetters fell off, and their feet were freed from the stocks to carry them forth out of prisons, accompanied by angels. They had power to win souls for Jesus by the thousand. They won them everywhere, in spite of governments, synagogues, priests, and all that rose up against them. They were a terror to governments, to councils, to priests, to formalists, to evil-doers, and a praise to them that were good.

POWER.

"Truly I am full of power by the spirit of the Lord."

—MICAH iii. 8.

POWER OF CONVICTION.

MEN have sought out many inventions. They have accomplished wonderful things. The least in the spiritual is greater than the greatest in the mental and material. The smallest thing that God ever did is greater than all the wonders that men have accomplished. God does only that which cannot possibly be wrought out by the best efforts and most ingenious schemes of men. Men may pray, exhort, sing, preach, and bring the heavens down around them by their faith, but God alone can touch the heart of the sinner. The soul of the sinner that has been stirred to its depths, so that he is ready to cry out in the agony of despair for mercy and salvation, has undergone a wonderful operation by the power of the Spirit of God. Conviction for sin, when wrought in the soul by the Spirit and Word of God, so that the sinner has become conscious of the whole weight of his actual sins, is a specific

work of God. God only can produce the effect.
We should not be surprised that so many mistake conviction for conversion. When the soul
is being deeply convinced of sin it undergoes a
radical change, which is perceptible, and so
much so that it is impossible to indulge in
habits which were formerly its supreme delight.

Those who have been in the habit of swearing, dare not utter an oath when conviction for
sin has taken possession of their souls. Many
have not been able to sleep at night on account
of the mighty workings of the Spirit in their
souls, the sorrows of death, and the pains of
hell having got hold of them. Some will pray
almost incessantly, and that is a new experience
for those who have not been accustomed to
engage in devotional exercises. Others have
become so enamored with religion and the
salvation of their souls, that they talk about it
almost without intermission. It is perfectly
natural for such persons to conclude that they
have met with the necessary change, when they
are not instructed in the plan of salvation.
The word of truth not being rightly divided

unto them, they are left to drift into error.
Many teachers have become so cold and formal
that they do not know when sinners are converted. They are slow to detect the difference
between conviction and conversion. Many cry
peace, peace, when there is no peace. God only
can say peace to the troubled heart. When
men cry peace, they are hindering the cause of
God, perverting the truth, and deluding the
inquirer.

THE POWER OF REGENERATION.

Regeneration is a miraculous manifestation of
divine power. The change wrought is great.
Old things pass away and all things become
new. New desires, intentions, thoughts, feelings, affections, heart, state, etc. Everything
new. Sins by the million forgiven. The greatest
sinner, when forgiven, stands as free from the
past, as if he never had broken a law of God.
A new state. Translated from the kingdom of
darkness into the kingdom of God's dear Son.
God for a Father, Jesus Christ for a Saviour
and Elder Brother, and the Holy Ghost for a

Comforter.   Condemnation all removed, "He that believeth is not condemned." "There is therefore now no condemnation to them that are in Christ Jesus." Justified from all things. There is nothing in the heavens above or on the earth beneath to condemn. Power is received over all inward and outward sin, and a consciousness that sin hath no more dominion, and a full persuasion that grace is all sufficient. Many who are regenerated conclude that the work is completed, and there is no need of any further change. True, they may feel no sin for a time, and believe that they never will. The change to them seems to be so complete, that they can see no possibility of anything moie being done.

It is perfectly natural for the regenerated to come to such a conclusion. The question comes to them does God half do a work. The answer in every case will be, No; He completes it. That is very true. He commenced to save the soul that was guilty and condemned on account of actual sins, and He completed that work. He did not commence to save the soul from inbred or Adamic sin, if He had He would have completed that work also. Why are they separated? Could God not do both at once? He could if He could do the work apart from us. But He could not do a work in us, apart from us. He saves from every sin that is repented of when faith takes hold of the promise. We repent of sin when it is shown to us by the Spirit. The sight of actual and inbred sin together would completely discourage any sinner. These two burdens together would completely paralyze any soul. The burden of actual sins is almost intolerable. The grace, light and power received at regeneration enables the soul to struggle with inbred sin, to repent and believe for entire sanctification.

THE POWER OF ENTIRE SANCTIFICATION.

Regeneration being a radical change, the whole being having been touched by it, what would be more natural than to conclude, that the work is completed, there being no consciousness of anything but love in the soul? The soul may be in this state for weeks, but when

6

provocation and temptation come, and the old Adam nature commences to rise, it becomes impossible at once to believe any longer that the work was perfected. It becomes at once apparent that there is need of a second change, if the soul is to be kept in perfect peace, always rejoicing in the fulness of the Gospel of Christ. Regeneration is sanctification commenced but not completed. There is a deep feeling of need in the hearts of those who have been regenerated, notwithstanding the soul has met with a very conscious change, and the Spirit's operation is felt with force and power, bearing witness to the work and sonship. The second change is greater than the first. It is deeper. The first overcomes the man of sin, the second casts him out. The change is a conscious one. It is attained by faith. It is instantaneous. It is the work of the Spirit. It can only be known by those who have experienced it. Others can only feel their need of it.

The repentance that precedes entire sanctification is deeper than that which was experienced before regeneration. The being is so thoroughly broken up, cleaned out and filled up, that it becomes difficult to think that there ever will be a feeling of need. Sin in its being having been completely eradicated from the soul, the language of the soul can never be less than "whiter than snow." The soul being so filled with peace, joy, love, and power, every want seems to be supplied. The entire sanctification of the nature is an experience that cannot be fathomed by any believer until the work has been wrought in the soul by the Holy Ghost, even then the half can never be told. This work permeates every faculty of the soul, and completely destroys every propensity and tendency toward evil. The roots of bitterness that spring up and defile many are all taken out, so that the soul has become a broken and emptied vessel for the Master's use made meet. When the being is thus cleansed, it is immediately filled with all the fulness of God's love. Love enters into every part of the being, so that God is loved with all the heart, mind, soul and strength, and the neighbor is loved with all the powers of the soul.

Entire sanctification takes hold of the intellect, as well as the moral and spiritual nature; it enters every faculty of the mind. It does more, it permeates, sets apart, quickens and energizes the whole. When the mind is under the operation of the Spirit, it must be active, and powerful, prepared for every exigency, and fully equipped for deeper researches into the truth, and clearer exposition, so that the Scriptures can be rightly divided. Entire sanctification not only reaches the mind and soul, but also the body. It goes through every member of the body. It destroys everything that is habitual, and gives perfect control over everything that is natural. This operation of the Spirit never destroys any natural faculty, passion or tendency of the soul. It brings everything that is natural under the direct and complete control of the will, so that the whole being is governed as designed by the Creator. Every faculty of mind and soul, and every member of the body are thoroughly purged from all the filthiness of the flesh and spirit, and holiness is being perfected in the fear of the Lord. This experience

will not be spasmodic, the faith that brings the
soul into that experience will keep it in that
state, so that it becomes the normal condition of
the soul. When the soul is in this state of
blessedness, it is easy to trust, and the natural
impulse will be to love God with all the heart.
It will be natural to believe that there is no
lack of power to accomplish all the will of God.
The soul thus blessed feels no lack, and is fully
persuaded that there is none. This blessing can
not be possibly less than the fulness of faith, the
fulness of peace, the fulness of joy, and the fulness of love, so that the soul is rejoicing with
joy unspeakable and full of glory. It is almost
impossible for a soul thus blessed to become
immediately conscious of his need of the baptism of power. If it is preached clearly and
definitely as the privilege of the sanctified, for
efficient service in the vineyard of the Lord
they will receive it at once. If a sanctified soul
will undertake to do at once all God would have
him do he will feel his need of the baptism of
the Holy Ghost and of fire.

THE BAPTISM OF THE HOLY GHOST.

There is power received when the soul is regenerated, and much more when it is sanctified wholly; still there is a special anointing of the Spirit, which is not received with either of these experiences. This baptism is to be "filled with power by the Spirit of the Lord, and of judgment, and of might, to declare unto Jacob his transgression, and to Israel his sin." It is power for service. To declare unto the sinner his transgression, and to the child of God the sin of his heart. It is judgment. It is power to say the right thing in such a way that the Spirit can carry it home to the heart of the sinner, and use it for the salvation of his soul, and the glory of God. The right thing may be said and nothing be accomplished. It is power to say the ·right thing at the right time, so that on every occasion the Spirit can carry it home with power to the heart. The Spirit can accomplish a mighty work when the material is at His disposal to be utilized. It is more than judgment, it is might. It is power to speak with a holy boldness. To say what God wants us to say just in the way it ought to be said. It is power to set home the truth with all the energy of the Holy Ghost, electrifying every faculty of the soul, which gives expression, life and power to the subject-matter. It is that strength of soul by which utterance can be given to the plainest truths, for the Spirit to accomplish the work. Truths that will cut in every direction that the Spirit can use to produce conviction, conversion and entire sanctification. Pentecostal power is the blood-bought right of all God's children. Those who have received it have power to accomplish wonderful things for the Lord Jesus. They can sound the depths of the most unbelieving heart. It is not salvation from sin, the soul that is not fully saved need not seek the baptism of power. It is the anointing which abideth. It empowers the soul with energy and might to pray, sing, exhort and win souls for Jesus. All who receive this baptism will be effectual workers in the vineyard of the Lord. It is power to win souls under every circumstance, and in every place. When God anoints it is power, and not something else. When He baptizes the soul with power to win others, it is not possible to fail; if the power that He gives is used there will be victory every time, and failure will be out of the question.

There are great mysteries connected with the Pentecost which have not been explained by any of the commentators or expositors of the past. Many of their expositions have only tended to mystify. The number who have thrown any light on the subject is very limited. They did not pretend to explain it. They had enough of grace and wisdom to leave alone that which God had not revealed unto them. All the leading doctrines of Scripture have been developed separately and specifically. It has been the divine order. There is a preparation in the minds of the people which is just as necessary to be developed as the doctrine itself. If the doctrine was developed and the minds of the people not prepared for it, they would not be capable of receiving it, and the mystery would thereby become greater. God has His own way, time and means for carrying out His purposes. His ways are past finding out. God must be His own interpreter, and He can make it plain. He chooses His own vessels, and because He chooses the weak things of this world to confound the mighty, and the foolish to condemn the wise, very frequently the message delivered is not accepted on account of the messenger. Those who ought to be the first to receive it, utterly reject it.

The doctrines of Christ have all met with much opposition, and not until their promulgators had enforced them, and were severely tested, were they received by the people who should have embraced them at once. He who will enforce a doctrine while it is new or unpopular, may expect to be criticised by his brethren, and lose the esteem of many friends. The majority of the people of God will look upon him with suspicion, and when he has done his best to make things plain, he will be called heterodox, if not dangerous in the extreme. To bear with such treatment at the hands of his brethren will test all the religion he has attained. The reformers and martyrs have been heroic and bold for Jesus; they counted not their lives dear that they might spread His redemptive glory. John Wesley suffered much misrepresentation from his brethren in the ministry while enforcing and spreading scriptural holiness throughout the land. If he had been moved by them, and had yielded to their cruel contempt, the millions who have been made partakers of that blessed experience would have remained in darkness.

When the nature is entirely sanctified, the soul is not weak, but has much power. When the soul has attained unto this experience it is full of love, peace and joy. The believer who is thus saved and filled, very naturally concludes that he has power, that it is not possible that God could perform another operation that would give him a greater efficiency for work. It is not so. The baptism of power is not received when the soul is being entirely sanctified. The promise is not given in that way. There have been no such experiences known in the history of the doctrine of holiness of heart and life. It is not natural to suppose that it would be so. People who are sick never expect the same medicine to destroy the power of disease, restore the system to perfect health, and give muscle force and power to prosecute work. They are generally well satisfied if they can secure one kind of medicine to shatter the power of the disease, and prevent it from working any farther into the system; another kind to restore the system to health by separating and driving from it all the lingering remains of the disease, so that the system is completely restored to a normal condition of health; and another to take hold of the dormant forces, which have been crippled by the cruel paralyzing power of disease, and bring the whole forces of the being into an active state. None ever expect a remedy for all of these in one. It would be unnatural. God's plan for saving the soul and qualifying it for usefulness is perfectly natural. He works along natural lines to give us all the possible insight into His operations.

When the soul is entirely sanctified it is restored to perfect health. Every faculty of soul and mind is full of health, but not necessarily or even possibly filled with power. Sin does much more than pollute every faculty of the soul and mind; it weakens, cripples, and paralyzes every faculty and fibre of the being. The baptism of the Holy Ghost takes hold of the whole being which has been sanctified wholly, and permeates every faculty and fibre of the being, so that the whole is set in motion. It feels like an electric shock. It runs along every nerve. It takes hold on every dormant force, and brings all into active, lively use. Every faculty is strengthened with might by the Spirit in the inner man, and filled with courage, strength and enthusiasm. The crippled faculties and forces are relaxed and electrified for actual and efficient service for the master.

WHAT IS POWER?

" Ye shall receive power after that the Holy Ghost is come upon you."

—ACTS i. 8.

WHAT IS POWER?

THE question very frequently arises what is this power and what effect does it have upon the children of God? Some have very materialistic ideas about it. So much so, that it seems to them to be something to be carried about that will explode and fell people to the ground. Others imagine that it would make them proud, and cause them to feel that they were a little in advance of their brethren and sisters in the Gospel. It produces no such effect. It does produce the opposite effect upon those who receive it.

POWER TO SEE OURSELVES.

It is power to see ourselves as God sees us. Power to see how weak we are, that we have no strength, that we are weaker than bruised reeds, that we need help every moment. Our strength consists in knowing how weak we are. "When I am weak, then am I strong." "My strength is made perfect in weakness." When we have seen how weak we are we will not press ourselves to the front. We will be satisfied to allow Jesus to go before us, and where He leads we will follow closely. After having seen our true inwardness with all our weaknesses and infirmities, we will not expect every person to say pleasant things about us. If people speak thus of us, we know their utterances are untrue; and should they say unkind things about us, our feelings are not hurt thereby. Our knowledge of ourselves prevents everything of that kind from taking place. Having come to know ourselves to be so much weaker than it is possible for others to know us, what they may say about us has no effect whatever. It is power to see under every circumstance that there is no possibility of us accomplishing anything of ourselves. Jesus will have the glory of our experiences. Whatsoever we do for the promotion of His cause, will be done with an eye single to His glory. It is to get into that position where Christ can be all and in all. It is to sink into the lowest depths of humility, where self will be out of sight, and Jesus can appear on the scene, as the fairest among ten thousand and the one altogether lovely. It is power to sink deeper, in order that we may rise higher. It is power to die daily to the world, to crucify the flesh with the affections and lust. It is to feel our need of inspiration in prayer, to be vividly conscious that mere words going up in the form of a petition, is only empty sound, and are not worth the breath expended. A form of prayer is an abomination to the Lord, and never rises higher than the head of the suppliant.

The soul baptized is deeply conscious that words, phrases, and rhetorical expressions are only the empty vaporings of the mind. Prayer must come from the heart in order to be heard, answered, or to remain as a memorial. The soul that has been baptized feels and knows that it is more than this. It is that divine energy in the soul by which we grasp the eternal, shake the gates of hell, open the heavens, bring salvation to men, and as the necessity of the case demands bring the presence of God and the glory of His power. It is power to feel and

7

understand that God must have the glory of our
experience, that He will not give His glory to
another.   The glory of God will be the continual aim and object.   Otherwise it would only
be empty noise.   It is to be fully persuaded
that God will help in giving expression to all
our feelings and frames of mind.   To undertake
would be to fail, unless God is directing our
steps and helping our judgment.   It is to know
that God will be present in every time of need.
It is to be alive to the truth that our influence
with and over others, without the immediate
presence of God, is so limited, that our very best
efforts to do them good will only prove to be
ineffectual.   It is to feel that we are broken and
emptied vessels, to be kept full for the Master's
use, so that God will be glorified by every aspi-
ration, by every intention, by every ambition
and capability of our souls.   It is God's opportunity for permeating, energizing, electrifying
and using every faculty of the mind and soul,
every member of the body and every fibre of
the being, for the promotion of His cause, the
conversion of His creatures, the sanctification of
His people, and the glory of His name.

IT IS POWER TO SEE JESUS.

It is more than power to see ourselves in our weaknesses, infirmities and utter inability to do anything of ourselves. It is more than power to see ourselves as God sees us. It is also power to see Jesus just as He is for us. We see that He is well qualified to meet every necessity of our peculiar circumstances and lives. It completely destroys the wish to be like some other person, in order that we might receive power, or be fully qualified for our special work in the vineyard of the Lord. It is power to see Jesus in the very moment that we get into distress and need special help. To see that He can fill every want our spirits feel, and more than make up for all our deficiencies in weaknesses, infirmities and ignorance. We can see in Him that which is adapted to our need under all our varied trials and efforts in peculiar places to do good.

While we are very keenly conscious of our weakness and inability, we are always alive to the great fact that our Saviour, Guide and

Leader is the Omnipotent Christ. It is power to behold Him everywhere present, as our Redeemer, our wall of defence, our sure support, our high tower, in all the might of His grace, to conquer and subdue all our foes, and keep us entire in all the will of our Master. It is to see Christ before us, over us, around us, underneath us, our Deliverer, and our Captain who never lost a battle. It is that manifestation of God's power in our souls, which makes that which was desired and longed for our present experience, in all its richness, beauty and power, to qualify us to do and to suffer. It makes doing and suffering the supreme delight of the soul. It clears away from the spiritual vision, all the mists and fogs that dim the sight, so that the invisible appears in sight and God is seen by mortal eye. It is a perfected vision of divine things, which have been purchased for us and perfectly adapted to our need.

POWER TO SEE JESUS WHEN PRAYING.

It is power to see Jesus when we pray, and prayer must then in every case be a power for good. The eye of faith need never lose the full apprehension. When the Christian is thus anointed, every time he bends his knees in prayer before God, the manifestation of His presence will be such, that all present will be mightily moved. Every time he prays his soul will be filled to its utmost capacity, and frequently the blessing will be pressed down, shaken together, and running over. When the Christian is baptized with the Spirit, and Jesus is kept in full view, it becomes an easy matter to shut the world, circumstances and surroundings out, so that God is held by a firm grasp, until the petition is granted and the soul goes up crying victory through the blood of the Lamb. When the soul is thus absorbed with the presence of Jesus and inspired by divine energy, it soars on the broad wings of faith, and takes in all the riches of His grace for the strengthening and vivifying of the whole being, for active and efficient service in the kingdom of Christ.

The presence of the Christ being fully realized under every circumstance, the soul immediately catches inspiration for supplication. The prayers are indited and so inspired by the Spirit that they never fall to the ground, they are always answered. The conscious presence of the Almighty Redeemer gives courage to the soul, to bear witness to the saving energy of the precious blood, and the power of the truth; so that the witness borne is the power of God to operate upon all who hear the message. With the living Christ in full view, the soul becomes bold to undertake and prosecute work in the vineyard of the Lord. Then failure is out of question. The soul will know nothing but victory. When Christ is in full vision, the soul knows nothing only to follow on, the attention cannot be secured by either men or devils. Where He leads the disposition is only to follow. Fighting will be a great delight, victory will be certain, salvation of souls realized, and the glory of God secured.

POWER TO SEE THE TRUTH.

This mighty baptism of the Spirit gives power to see the truth as it is in Jesus Christ. The whole truth as essential to our completeness, and qualification for special efforts, for the

glory of God, in the salvation of souls. It is
more than power to see the truth and the whole
truth, it is power to rightly divide the word of
truth, and appropriate for our necessities, as
well as in extremities, that portion of it that is
adapted for each occasion. Truths which were
formerly familiar and presented to our need
much comfort and consolation will sparkle with
new beauties, and are transformed from the
lifeless letter of the word into the quick and
powerful word that gives light and life. This
baptism gives an insight into the Word of God
which cannot be attained in any other way.
An extensive knowledge of the Scriptures can
be acquired by historical research, by study in
their original languages, and the development
of their doctrines ; but all this is limited in its
power to grasp the deep and inner meaning of
the Word, compared with that which is revealed
by the illumination of the pentecostal baptism
of the Spirit. It is power to see the truth in
its beauty and simplicity. The Bible will be no
longer a sealed book, but will be a storehouse of
knowledge, where the soul can draw in abun-

dance for all exigencies, and always be fully equipped for the work in every place, and under every circumstance. It is power to see every command, and delight in obeying them. The promises will be clearer and seem to be much more numerous, and will throb with new life, power and glory. This power is that energy of the soul by which is seen and accepted, not only all that the promise contains, but appropriates all that is in it for the purpose to which the promise was given. The whole truth in its adaptation for peculiar, as well as practical purposes, can and will be utilized when it is thus known and received. The anointing of the Holy Ghost abideth and gives visions and revelations, which are mighty under God for the spread of the Gospel, and the sanctification of the believers in Christ. " I will pour out of my Spirit upon all flesh : and your sons and your daughters shall prophesy, and your young men shall see visions."

POWER TO PREVAIL.

It is power to pray for what we need in such a way that we have not to ask the second time for the same blessing. It is power to take hold of God in such a way that we feel that we are wrestling with Him. It is a Jacob-like spirit. It may be much more than Jacob had, but certainly it cannot be less. He who is fully baptized with the Holy Ghost is within reach of heaven's batteries, and can, without effort, touch and immediately feel the electrifying power of the Spirit permeating and filling every fibre of his soul with divine, vivifying energy, and thrilling every nerve and tissue of his physical organization. When the soul is thus humiliated, overcome and controlled by the power of the Spirit, prayers are indited and so fully inspired that they will take hold of God the Father, through God the Son, by the energy of God the Holy Ghost. One hath said that it is a God wrestling with a God. Hell will shake, heaven will open, streams of blessing will flow, and the soul will be enlarged and filled with all the fulness of the blessing of the Gospel of Christ. The soul fully baptized with the Holy Ghost never whines for bread and water, but can eat and drink, and be satisfied. There is no strength or energy spent in seeking; no loss of vital force; no loss of time. The anointed are always ready for the fight, and fully equipped with the whole armor of God. Prayer has become the vital breath, the watchword, the native air and the energy of the soul.

The prayers of the anointed never fall from the lip, never hang around the head, but go straight up to the throne. When a Christian is thus anointed, he is never satisfied with a small portion. The hunger and thirst for spiritual food has been greatly intensified. The soul will continually expand and follow after greater manifestations of power. One baptism only prepares the soul for another and greater, and gives power to claim and believe for it, and use it for the glory of God when received. The power increases as the capability of the soul expands.

POWER TO APPROPRIATE.

It is power to believe. There is no lingering doubt left in the mind. No misgivings. The faith of the baptized soul readily grasps all the promises. It is power to see many promises more clearly, which were previously obscure to the eye of faith. Faith having become a power to appropriate, the soul continues to be filled with all the fulness of God. The power to believe having become perfectly natural, the moment that the desire flows from the soul, faith receives all that is desired. Trusting is like breathing, there is an outward and inward flow which is perfectly free, without any impediment whatever. The power of faith having become so enlarged, new possibilities become apparent continually, and faith will take in all that is revealed by the baptisms of the Holy Ghost. There will be no conscious effort to believe. The baptism of power can be no less than the fulness of faith ; it is much more. The baptized soul never waits, and is never in suspense for a blessing. The baptism of power brings the soul into perfect harmony with God, and His time and ways will, in every case and under every circumstance, be acceptable. The *now* of the Gospel having been accepted, the *waiting* of the law will be considered a thing of the past The soul will live in the present tense of the Gospel. The promises will be received as they are, not in the future, but in the present tense. The power of the truth will immediately be felt. The force of the truth will be realized, that all things are possible to him that believeth. The soul will never be lean, living on half rations, but will always be filled, and delighting itself in fatness. The power of faith will continually expand. It will become broad and far-reaching. It will be as broad as the truth of God. Faith reaches up to God, it soars to the eternal city, it transcends reason, it moves and operates only in the region of the spiritual.

> " Faith, mighty faith, the promise sees,
>   And looks to that alone ;
>   Laughs at impossibilities,
>   And cries, ' It shall be done !' "

POWER AND ITS RELATIONS.

" *Ye shall be witnesses unto Me.*'

—ACTS i. 8.

POWER RELATIVE TO OUR
BRETHREN.

THE baptism of power is not exclusively confined to the individual who has received it. It has a relation to the Church of God. It is not only power to see ourselves, it is power to see our brethren and sisters in the Church. The cold, formal, dead condition of many professors of religion, especially when accompanied by worldliness or some other form of sin, as it generally is, is a deplorable sight to behold when our spiritual vision has been clarified. The sight is saddening, and when persisted in, becomes disgusting. Those who have seen it, cease to wonder why the Lord said that He would spue the lukewarm out of His mouth. It is most blessed that the anointing gives power to see our brethren and sisters in this deplorable state. It is more deplorable when they are in this cold, formal state, and none of their teachers have been anointed with eye salve to see them. If none can see, then none can help. Medical men who do not understand the nature of a disease, may prescribe powders, tonics, etc., and out of one hundred kinds of medicine, there is probably only one kind that will effect a cure. One kind would relieve, another would irritate, and another would stupefy, etc., but only one chance out of one hundred for life. Any one of these hundred drugs may be given, while there is only one that would be effectual. There is a possibility of doing good and helping our brethren and sisters, and for every one we help, we hinder ninety-nine others, until such times as our eyes are opened, to see the kind of help they need from us. When we have received the anointing that abideth, we have power to see how to lead them out of the old ruts which they have fallen into. It is power to pray for them, to believe for them, and to rightly divide the word of truth, giving each the necessary portion to lead him into light. It is power to see the possibility of all being led into the fulness of light, and being baptized with the Holy Ghost

and with fire. It is more than this. It is power
to lead them into this experience. Once it has
become the language of the soul there is no
difficulty in telling it to others. It can be sent
home to them with such force and power that
they cannot resist it, they must yield to be led
in a way that they know not.

POWER RELATIVE TO THE SINNER.

It is more than power to see the state of the
professors of religion around us ; it is power to
see the unsaved, the perishing masses out of
Christ. When we can see sinners by the million
on the verge of the pit, and tumbling into hell
by the thousand, our souls will be stirred to
their deepest emotions. The sight is terrific.
How they are blinded by the god of this world !
How many fetters binding their souls to hell !
It is power to see them slipping down, and none
caring for them—none to rescue. Many professing to have the light, but none letting it
shine for these benighted creatures. Oh, the
the darkness, how it thickens, like the brooding
of despair. It is power to see this dense, thick

darkness. It is power to penetrate it, to see into the thick darkness. This is what it is, to be baptized with the Holy Ghost. It gives a clear vision of those who are groping in this dense, thick darkness. The sight is appalling. It commands all our sympathy. This blessed eye-salve clears away the mists, so that the soul can see to the very verge of the pit. We hear the moans, the weeping, the wailing, and the gnashing of the teeth of the damned of all the ages. The soul that has its vision thus cleared of all mists has a wonderful insight into the souls of those who have not yet passed over, but are ripening on the very verge, ready to fall headlong into the abyss. It is power to see the weakness and helplessness of the fallen, that they have no strength, that unless they are helped, and that speedily, that there is no hope for them. How many there are professing to see who are in gross darkness! Stepping around with an air of politeness, singing and testifying that they are glad that they are saved to wear a crown ; but perfectly indifferent regarding the salvation of the perishing. Not able to see and

not caring to see them in their lost and perishing condition. God Almighty the Father, Jesus
Christ the Saviour, Holy Ghost the Comforter,
give the anointing to the Church that will clear
away the mists, so that the perishing may be
rescued. Come, great Spirit, come and give the
anointing which abideth.

POWER TO SYMPATHIZE WITH THE LOST.

It is more than power to see sinners in their
fallen and lost condition away from God. It is
power to sympathize with them in their peculiar and particular circumstances. It is sympathy that sinners need. They receive very
little, and they need much. Most professors of
religion look down upon sinners; when they
have fallen, what they call low, they give them
no encouragement whatever. Sinners do not
need that kind of treatment at the hands of
professors of religion. They receive plenty of
that sort from their own class. God hath
designed that they should have perfect sympathy from His people, He holds them duty-
bound to sympathize with the sinner, and

does and will not justify them in doing otherwise. Sinners expect sympathy from the
people of God, and when they do not receive it
they lose faith in their profession. The believer
who is fully baptized with the Holy Ghost and
with fire is in perfect sympathy with all
classes, grades, stations and degrees of sinners,
and is thoroughly prepared to help them out of
darkness into the marvellous light. The soul
that is fully aroused, and is in sympathy and
touch with all, can arouse a chord of sympathy
in the hearts of the unsaved around him. Like
begets like. The Christian who is in perfect
sympathy with the sinner will produce a like
feeeling of sympathy in the sinner's heart for
the means which are being used for his salvation. He will be drawn out into perfect
sympathy with every look, every word, and
every effort put forth to rescue him from the
destroyer's cruel power. When the sympathy
has become perfectly mutual the work has
become comparatively easy and the possibility
of it being effected has become an absolute
certainty. He becomes at once passive and

teachable. He only wants to know what he must do in order to be saved. When the Church of God is baptized with the Holy Ghost and fire, sinners will be converted by the thousand, where they are only fancifully converted by the dozen now. It is this baptism of power that is going to bring the world to Jesus.

IT IS CHARITY THAT NEVER FAILETH.

It is power to love the poor sinner, as we love our own souls. This is the only way of reaching the masses who are perishing. This way is effectual without exception. It takes love to reach the wanderer, and bring him back to the fold. While the sinner is conscious that no person loves him he will not try to reform. He will sink lower, believing that it is impossible for him to rise, or do any better than he has been doing. There are many to draw him down, and he knows it. He becomes completely discouraged. He immediately concludes that no person loves him, that no man cares for his soul. What does such a person need, but some one to love him, and let him know it? When he becomes fully conscious that all have not given him up, that some care for him, he takes courage, and is delighted to know that he is not utterly cast off. Does any person love me? Can it be so? are questions that come to him. When he is caused to believe it, the very thought itself will melt and move his obdurate heart. Love carries out the soul by sweet constraint after the perishing, until they are influenced, induced, persuaded and won.

Love is sure to win, it is stronger than the human heart, stronger than hell, stronger than the devil, and mighty to subdue and conquer and save all who are reached by it. It never fails. It knows nothing but victory. The soul that is baptized with the Holy Ghost will be an efficient worker in the vineyard of the Lord. The love will constrain. The love of God must be manifested to the sinner, by those who profess to have it shed abroad in their hearts, by the Holy Ghost given unto them. This is God's way of making the sinner conscious of His great love for him. He may fear and have a dread of God as the Omnipotent, but he can only know of His love as it is manifested to him. The anointing of the Holy Ghost gives power to those who receive it, to manifest the love of God to the perishing masses around them. This is God's method of reaching the people. He commenced in that way on the day of Pentecost. He baptized one hundred and twenty with the Holy Ghost, and out of the fulness of love, they had power to tell it to the masses, and they were converted by the thousand.

Before the apostles received this mighty baptism of the Spirit they were very ordinary preachers of the Gospel, their efforts to reach the masses were almost a failure, they did not move many. Their love had not become intense. It lacked the moving power, the melting energy that belongs to those whose souls have reached a white heat by the fire of the Holy Ghost. When they were baptized with the Holy Ghost, they had love enough to reach sinners by the thousand. It gave them a bold-ness for Jesus, and the courage of their convictions. They were willing to endure all things for the sake of the cause of Christ, and there was not anything too hard for them. The impelling power of the fulness of the love of God completely overcame them, and carried them through every battle to sure and complete victory. Their love for the cause of God and the salvation of the perishing, made it a delight for them to go to prison, to bear the lashes, the fetters, the stocks and the confinement. It did more than that for them, they had power to sing praises at midnight and arouse the prisoners, and cause the earth to quake, the prison doors to swing open, to get gaolers and their families converted to God. It made the service of God a supreme delight under every circumstance. They served God, obeyed His voice, and did His bidding ; not because they feared Him, not because it was their duty to do so, but for the love they had for Him, and the joy it afforded them to bring glory to His name. They counted not their lives dear, and were ready to die for the cause of God. Death in any form had no dread for them. The fervency of their love for Christ, and His redemptive

glory, made it their supreme delight to suffer
for Him.   They had no dread of the grave, the
cross, the block, the stones, or the faggots.
They were kept by the power of God, through
faith, ready to be revealed.   The love of God
was sweeter than honey in the honey-comb, and
dearer that life itself.   By the power of this
love they could cheerfully and joyfully die for
the cause of the Redeemer, and pray for their
murderers.

> " Angels assist our mighty joys,
>   Strike all your harps of gold ;
> But when you've raised your highest notes,
>   His love can ne'er be told."

POWER TO PREVAIL FOR SINNERS.

It is power to pray for sinners, and thus
make them feel keenly their need of Christ.   It
is that sympathy and love for sinners that gives
us the capability to plead their cases at the
throne of grace.   It is power to step into their
shoes and plead for them with God through the
mediation of Jesus Christ.   When the believer
is baptized with the Holy Ghost, he can take

the sinner upon his heart, and hold him before
the throne of grace, until the warming rays of
the Sun of Righteousness will warm and melt his
icy-cold heart. When the sinner is thus moved
and attracted by the Christ, the Holy Ghost
will produce conviction so deep and pungent,
that he will cry out as out of the belly of hell.
It is power to get down in the mud underneath
the sinner, and bear him up before the throne,
until the pains of hell get hold of him and he
finds trouble and sorrow. When believers pray
in the Spirit after being baptized with the Holy
Ghost, they can so move and trouble the sinners
that they cannot eat, sleep, or work. They can
make it so hard for sinners to go to hell, that
they will choose to turn and seek salvation.
Their prayers never fall to the ground, they
always reach the throne of God, and the answer
comes speedily. They do not pray blindly, their
prayers are indited by the Holy Ghost; they
pray under direct inspiration. When the Spirit
has been received in His fulness, He indites and
inspires all the prayers and supplications. The
soul that is baptized with the Holy Ghost does

not harp on the one string that sinners have wills and will not yield. They know that sinners have wills, but they do not believe that they are omnipotent; they bend and break their wills with their prayers, faith, appeals and exhortations. There is a kind of omnipotence in prayer which has always been irresistible. It will break through the walls of difficulty. Those who do not believe in the omnipotence of prayer will stand on the other side of the wall and whine, while those who believe go right through it. Prayer climbs the ladder, throws down the wall, removes the mountains, sounds the unbelieving heart, and puts to flight the armies of the aliens. The soul that is thoroughly baptized with the Holy Ghost knows no limits to the divine operations, and will venture to undertake anything for God.

THE SOUL-WINNER.

The baptism of the Holy Ghost prepares all who receive it to be efficient workers in the vineyard of the Lord. It is power to win souls for the Lord Jesus by the hundred. There are many workers, but there are few soul-winners. One immediate effect of this baptism is the power to get hold of some perishing soul and lead him to Jesus. There will be a power in the experience which when told will immediately prick the sinner's heart, and lead him to inquire what he must do to be saved. Preachers of the Gospel who have been anointed will win souls by the hundred, and some who have more than ordinary ability will win them by the thousand. A Church which has been baptized with the Holy Ghost, will win souls in the ordinary services of the sanctuary, and will have a constant revival of religion. It makes all who receive it practical and successful workers in the vineyard. It is not possible for those who are under the power of the Spirit to be at ease in Zion. There will be no disposition to be idle. There will be an ambition to accomplish much for the glory of God. It is power to see how to win the most wicked sinner for Jesus, to see the possibilities of divine grace. It is more than power to see how to win sinners, it is power to lead them into the light. None will be too hard,

all things will be possible to the believer. Those
who have been given up and cast off, will be
brought safely into the fold.   Drunkards, blas-
phemers, Sabbath breakers, gamblers, etc., will
be rescued by the hundred.   The apostles did
not know the extent of their power after the
day of Pentecost.   They were irresistible.   They
could win souls everywhere in spite of the
world, in spite of the devil, in spite of formalists, and in spite of governments.   There was no
power that could withstand them.   After the
day of Pentecost they could get them converted
by the thousand to the Lord Jesus, where they
could not get them converted by the score previous to that day.   The pentecost was to them,
what it is to all who receive it now, a special
anointing for service.

POWER TO LEAD.

It is more than power to win souls for Jesus ;
it is power to keep them in the service of God
faithful and true.   The trouble in the churches
to-day is, not to get people converted, but to
keep them after they have been converted.

The great majority of those who have been received lose their faith, love and zeal, and become backsliders. There being no place to stand on the road to heaven, they must either go forward or go back. When preachers, teachers, and leaders have never advanced or taken higher ground themselves, they are unqualified to lead the children of the Church to a higher plane of religious experience. The number who will rise superior to their teachers are but few, a large majority never hope to do anything of the kind. The believer who has been baptized with the Holy Ghost has taken higher ground, and has become qualified to lead others to the same rich experience. Having travelled over the ground, they fully understand where and how to lead others. The experience itself is the only qualification for directing the steps of others. The babes in Christ can be guided with care and certainty, and are not left to grope and wander in the wilderness, when their teachers have been baptized with the Holy Ghost. They will lead them into the blessed possession of the promised land. The baptism of power enables those who have received it to lead the children of God to realize their need of a second great change. It is power to so sound the depths of the human heart, that the Spirit can produce the conviction for the second change so deep and pungent, that the blessing must be sought and attained. It is power to lead them on in that experience for the anointing of the Spirit for service. They will be led to see their privilege in Christ Jesus, and receive frequent baptisms, so that they will expand and develop under the mighty operations of the Spirit. Thus they are led on from strength to strength, until they become giants for God. They will have no ups nor downs, and will never have to cry my leanness, but will live on the fat of the land. This is Bible and apostolic religion, and God's method of saving a lost and ruined world. Come, oh, come, great Spirit, come and baptize us now.

HISTORY.

" *Stephen, full of faith and power, did great wonders and miracles among the people.*"

ACT᷄ vi.

HISTORY OF THE DOCTRINE.

MOST professors of religion know no difference between the blessing of entire sanctification and the baptism of the Holy Ghost. The majority of modern teachers believe that they are received simultaneously, that when the soul is sanctified that pentecostal power is received. Others have invented a theory which puts the soul that accepts it in possession of the Holy Ghost as a guide who will infallibly conduct, control and lead them in all things, independent of reason, judgment, or the Word of God. This guide is received once for all at the time the soul is entirely sanctified. Those who accept this theory must reject the teaching of Scripture, that the Holy Ghost leads all who have been converted from the moment that they receive the Spirit of adoption. "If any man have not the Spirit of Christ, he is none of of His." "As many as are led by the Spirit of God they are the sons of God." The Holy

Ghost will guide the soul into all the truth
essential to salvation, from the moment that
Christ has been received as the Saviour, if the
believer will follow the guidance of the Spirit.
He does not absolutely guide, so that there is no
possibility of God's children making mistakes.
He helps all the powers of the intellect, and
does not supersede any power of the mind.
These faculties are designed to be developed by
the operation of the Spirit. The Holy Ghost is
received when the soul is converted, and abides
in the soul the infallible testimony that all
actual sins are forgiven. He also bears testimony in the soul that the nature is entirely
sanctified when that blessing is received, and
will empower all who seek the baptism of power
for service. Those who are not led by the
Spirit from the time they are converted are
backsliders. When they receive the Spirit they
are only restored. This is how the doctrine of
holiness is brought into disrepute. Those who
have this experience are weaklings, being cut
off by their theory from the baptism of the
Holy Ghost. Many of them have nothing more

than the profession. God did not design that
His children should be weaklings, and thus give
the lie to their profession. He made provision
for His children to have power. Jesus came to
take away our sins and give us many baptisms
of the Holy Ghost. He baptizeth with the
Holy Ghost. It is not just one baptism. It is
one baptism after another increasing in power,
as the capacity for receiving it has been
developed. The verb " baptizeth " is in the
present indefinite tense, expressive of continued
or repeated action, the same tense as "believeth."
Each baptism received prepares the soul for
receiving a greater one the next time. The
more frequently the baptism is received, the
greater the hungering and thirsting become.
Those who have received it once know what it
is, how they received it, and where it came
from ; and they always have a consciousness
that it can be received again in greater power.
Just as they use what they have received they
will get more, and when they undertake great
things for the Lord Jesus, the baptism will be
accordingly great. There is no limit to it, just

as there is none to the power of God. He gives according to the faith of those who receive it. Thus the people of God can be equal to every occasion, and know nothing but victory. It does not make all who receive it alike, any more than it enables all who receive it to accomplish all that God designed that they should.

God intended that we should do so much more than any of us ever expected to do, that we are surprised at ourselves after we have been anointed to see what wonders we can accomplish for the Master. It enables those who receive it to do all that God intended that they should do. It makes the very best possible out of the material in us for the glory of God. There are other teachers of holiness who affirm that the apostles and disciples were not converted until the day of Pentecost. There is as much reason in one as in the other. There is no Scripture to support either theories. Did none of the patriarchs or prophets ever get converted? Were there none converted until the day of Pentecost? If so, why not the apostles of the Lord Jesus? Could the Lord Jesus cast

a legion of devils out of a man and yet not be
able to save him ?   Jesus saved all who came to
Him seeking salvation.   To affirm the contrary
is to pervert the Scriptures.   The Scriptures
present regeneration, entire sanctification, and
the baptism of power, as separate, definite blessings to be definitely sought and obtained by
faith.   Those who hold that they are one, must
have come to that conclusion without a proper
investigation of the subject.   It may never have
occurred to them that there was such a blessing
held forth as attainable, until their opinions had
become fixed and they had committed themselves to some erroneous theory.   Once a theory
has been accepted, be it right or wrong, most
people are slow to abandon it.

Commentators who are sound in Scripture
exegesis and acknowledged authorities on points
of doctrine, have been careful in expressing
themselves on these point, they have kept them
separate, and have not changed the divine order
nor destroyed the spirit of the truth as it is in
Jesus.   Most writers on the subject of holiness
have been careful and explicit, they have not

attempted to make holiness and the baptism of the Holy Ghost one and the same blessing. What God hath set apart they have not ventured to join together. When we speak of writers on the subject of holiness we need not mention any except John Wesley. While there have been many books written on this subject, especially in modern times, there has been nothing new except that which is unsound. There is nothing written that is scriptural that could not be read out of John Wesley's works.

These modern writers have been obliged to quote directly from John Wesley when they wanted to prove a point and make it acceptable to the public mind. Take from these books all the quotations from John Wesley, and there would be very little left worth reading. They have done nothing more than mystify that which was made plain by Wesley. In many instances we are obliged to read pages of these books to find what might be had by reading a single paragraph of Wesley's writing. Wesley is clear, pointed and scriptural. Every sentence is full of clear light on the subject, and scrip-

tural in its order.   Everything in its right
place, logical and close, clearly cut, directing the
way, so that none may be deceived, who are
seeking after the truth, and are intent on finding it.   John Wesley's writings on the subject
of holiness are clear, full and explicit.   They
have stood all the criticisms that have been
offered, and are acknowledged, by all teachers of
holiness, to be the standard.   Criticism at
various times has only caused the masses to
read what he wrote and learn for themselves,
that his teaching is based upon Scripture, that
he proved every point from the Word of God.
Wesley taught holiness by the commands,
prayers and promises in the Word, given to
God's people.   He selected commands from the
Old and New Testaments, but did not use any
that were given by the Lord Jesus to the
apostles regarding the Pentecost.   They were
told to tarry in the city of Jerusalem until they
would be endued with power from on high.
Wesley did not quote this command given by
the Lord Jesus to the disciples.   The question
is why did he not ?   Simply because he knew

that they had received holiness, and this command was for the special anointing for service, which they received on the day of Pentecost.

Wesley taught that holiness was salvation from inbred sin, and he knew that the disciples were not told to wait for cleansing. He collected and quoted prayers that had been offered up for the entire sanctification of God's people, but did not intimate that any of these prayers were answered on the day of Pentecost. The Saviour had prayed for the entire sanctification of His disciples. (John xvii. 17.) He could have showed that the disciples had received that blessing on the day of Pentecost, if he had believed that entire sanctification and the Pentecost were one and the same blessing. There is no Scripture that would have suited his purpose so well, or that would have made his points so strong as these commands and prayers, if it had been right for him to have used them, to establish the doctrine. He had many good promises from both the Old and New Testaments to prove his points, but none of them were so adapted, or so full of force, as the promises given to the apostles, if it were true that He was promising holiness. "Ye shall be baptized with the Holy Ghost not many days hence." "Ye shall receive power after that the Holy Ghost is come upon you."

These promises and their fulfilment on the day of Pentecost would have proved at once that the blessing was instantaneous, and not a gradual work. The history of the men who have professed to have received the blessing of entire sanctification, would be sufficient proof that there is a difference between entire sanctification and the baptism of power. They have not had the power that the apostles had for service. They have not achieved as great victories for the Lord Jesus. Their efforts have been comparatively fruitless, especially may it be said of holiness professors of modern times.

The number who have had similar power and success are few. John Wesley, Whitefield, Finney, Edwards, Cahey and a few others, especially of Wesley's preachers, have had similar success in the work, to that which attended the labor of the apostles. Dr. Burwash has said that John Wesley was entirely sanctified at the time that he supposed that he was converted. We have strong reasons for believing this to be the truth, his life for some time previous to that date was everything that could be expected of any minister of the Gospel in self-denial, in fasting, in private devotion, and in practical efforts for the salvation of souls. He would put to shame many professors of holiness of this century, if they would compare their lives with his. When he received what he called entire sanctification, it must have been the baptism of the Holy Ghost, as they received it on the day of Pentecost. One thing is certain, if John Wesley did not receive something more than entire sanctification then, there are none who receive this blessing now, and those who profess to have received it are either deluded or they are impostors. About one half of the Methodist ministry profess to be in the enjoyment of this great blessing of entire sanctification, and if one quarter of that number are in possession of it, then it is certain that John Wesley had something more than that which is called entire sanctification. There is not one out of every hundred, who profess to enjoy this blessing, as self-denying and devoted as John Wesley was.

John Wesley was blessed with such an overwhelming sense of God's presence and power as Christians do not expect to receive in these modern times.

"The first time I saw Mr. B. was June 2, 1758, but I scarce thought of him again till June 7, as I was walking up to Luton-Down. There an awful sense of God's presence fell upon me, and my voice grew louder and louder, in proportion to the joy of my soul, with a strong impulse to pray for the success of Mr. B.'s labors. And such a foresight did the Lord give me of what He was bringing to pass through his ministry, that I was quite overwhelmed for near an hour, till my voice was lost, and only tears remained." *Journal*, July 23, 1759, Vol. II., page 507.

This would be called excitement, hysteria, or wild-fire by most professors of holiness in this century. Most preachers of holiness would not permit their hearers to profess to have received such a manifestation of God's power. If during some of their prayer-meetings, some one should be anointed as here expressed in the words of John Wesley as his own definite experience, he would soon have the room to himself, for both preacher and people would run out of the place. John Wesley received power to preach the Gospel of Christ. When he preached the hardest of sinners were mightily moved to repentance, they fell as dead men under the sound of his voice, which was electrified by the baptism of the Holy Ghost. Conviction was so deep and pungent, that their groans and cries for mercy and salvation could be heard afar off. He had pentecostal power, and under his preaching saints and sinners would fall down as dead men, while he described the terrors of the law, and the love of God in Christ Jesus, in redemption and salvation from sin. He was pre-eminently apostolic in faith, in love, in zeal, in enthusiasm, and in power to sound the depths of the unbelieving heart. He could win the blasphemer, the drunkard, the mocker, and those who would go for the purpose of breaking up his meetings would fall as dead men while he preached to them the Gospel.

There is not one kind of holiness for John Wesley, and another kind for the rest of us. It is certain that holiness and the baptism of the Holy Ghost and fire will not make us all Wesleys in natural ability, or endow us with certain mental or physical powers that are indispensable for the accomplishment of certain lines of work in the Master's vineyard.

Those who are sanctified wholly and baptized with the Holy Ghost and fire, can accomplish all that God designs that they should, as fully as John Wesley did.

TITLES in THIS SERIES

geles, 1925), *AROUND THE WORLD BY FAITH, WITH SIX WEEKS IN THE HOLY LAND* (Los Angeles, n. d.), *TWO YEARS MISSION WORK IN EUROPE JUST BEFORE THE WORLD WAR, 1912-14* (Los Angeles, [1926])

6. Boardman, W. E., *THE HIGHER CHRISTIAN LIFE* (Boston, 1858)

7. Girvin, E. A., *PHINEAS F. BRESEE: A PRINCE IN ISRAEL* (Kansas City, Mo., [1916])

8. Brooks, John P., *THE DIVINE CHURCH* (Columbia, Mo., 1891)

9. RUSSELL KELSO CARTER ON "FAITH HEALING." R. Kelso Carter, *THE ATONEMENT FOR SIN AND SICKNESS* (Boston, 1884) *"FAITH HEALING" REVIEWED AFTER TWENTY YEARS* (Boston, 1897)

10. Daniels, W. H., *DR. CULLIS AND HIS WORK* (Boston, [1885])

11. HOLINESS TRACTS DEFENDING THE MINISTRY OF WOMEN. Luther Lee, *"WOMAN'S RIGHT TO PREACH THE GOSPEL; A SERMON, AT THE ORDINATION OF REV. MISS ANTOINETTE L. BROWN, AT SOUTH BUTLER, WAYNE COUNTY, N. Y., SEPT. 15, 1853"* (Syracuse, 1853) *bound with* B. T. Roberts, *ORDAINING WOMEN* (Rochester, 1891) *bound with* Catherine (Mumford) Booth, *"FEMALE MINISTRY; OR, WOMAN'S RIGHT TO PREACH THE GOSPEL . . ."* (London, n. d.) *bound with* Fannie (McDowell) Hunter, *WOMEN PREACHERS* (Dallas, 1905)

12. LATE NINETEENTH CENTURY REVIVALIST TEACHINGS ON THE HOLY SPIRIT. D. L. Moody, *SECRET POWER OR THE SECRET OF SUCCESS IN CHRISTIAN LIFE AND*

WORK (New York, [1881]) *bound with* J. Wilbur Chapman, *RECEIVED YE THE HOLY GHOST?* (New York, [1894]) *bound with* R. A. Torrey, *THE BAPTISM WITH THE HOLY SPIRIT* (New York, 1895 & 1897)

13. SEVEN "JESUS ONLY" TRACTS. Andrew D. Urshan, *THE DOCTRINE OF THE NEW BIRTH, OR, THE PERFECT WAY TO ETERNAL LIFE* (Cochrane, Wis., 1921) *bound with* Andrew Urshan, *THE ALMIGHTY GOD IN THE LORD JESUS CHRIST* (Los Angeles, 1919) *bound with* Frank J. Ewart, *THE REVELATION OF JESUS CHRIST* (St. Louis, n. d.) *bound with* G. T. Haywood, *THE BIRTH OF THE SPIRIT IN THE DAYS OF THE APOSTLES* (Indianapolis, n. d.) *DIVINE NAMES AND TITLES OF JEHOVAH* (Indianapolis, n. d.) *THE FINEST OF THE WHEAT* (Indianapolis, n. d.) *THE VICTIM OF THE FLAMING SWORD* (Indianapolis, n. d.)

14. THREE EARLY PENTECOSTAL TRACTS. D. Wesley Myland, *THE LATTER RAIN COVENANT AND PENTECOSTAL POWER* (Chicago, 1910) *bound with* G. F. Taylor, *THE SPIRIT AND THE BRIDE* (n. p., [1907?]) *bound with* B. F. Laurence, *THE APOSTOLIC FAITH RESTORED* (St. Louis, 1916)

15. Fairchild, James H., *OBERLIN: THE COLONY AND THE COLLEGE, 1833-1883* (Oberlin, 1883)

16. Figgis, John B., *KESWICK FROM WITHIN* (London, [1914])

17. Finney, Charles G., *LECTURES TO PROFESSING CHRISTIANS* (New York, 1837)

18. Fleisch, Paul, *DIE MODERNE GEMEINSCHAFTS-BEWEGUNG IN DEUTSCHLAND* (Leipzig, 1912)

19. SIX TRACTS BY W. B. GODBEY. *SPIRITUAL GIFTS AND GRACES* (Cincinnati, [1895]) *THE RETURN OF JESUS* (Cincinnati, [1899?]) *WORK OF THE HOLY SPIRIT* (Louisville, [1902]) *CHURCH—BRIDE—KINGDOM* (Cincinnati, [1905]) *DIVINE HEALING* (Greensboro, [1909]) *TONGUE MOVEMENT, SATANIC* (Zarephath, N. J., 1918)

20. Gordon, Earnest B., *ADONIRAM JUDSON GORDON* (New York, [1896])

21. Hills, A. M., *HOLINESS AND POWER FOR THE CHURCH AND THE MINISTRY* (Cincinnati, [1897])

22. Horner, Ralph C., *FROM THE ALTAR TO THE UPPER ROOM* (Toronto, [1891])

23. McDonald, William and John E. Searles, *THE LIFE OF REV. JOHN S. INSKIP* (Boston, [1885])

24. LaBerge, Agnes N. O., *WHAT GOD HATH WROUGHT* (Chicago, n. d.)

25. Lee, Luther, *AUTOBIOGRAPHY OF THE REV. LUTHER LEE* (New York, 1882)

26. McLean, A. and J. W. Easton, *PENUEL; OR, FACE TO FACE WITH GOD* (New York, 1869)

27. McPherson, Aimee Semple, *THIS IS THAT: PERSONAL EXPERIENCES SERMONS AND WRITINGS* (Los Angeles, [1919])

28. Mahan, Asa, *OUT OF DARKNESS INTO LIGHT* (London, 1877)

29. THE LIFE AND TEACHING OF CARRIE JUDD MONTGOMERY Carrie Judd Montgomery, *"UNDER HIS WINGS": THE STORY OF MY LIFE* (Oakland,

[1936]) Carrie F. Judd, *THE PRAYER OF FAITH* (New York, 1880)

30. THE DEVOTIONAL WRITINGS OF PHOEBE PALMER Phoebe Palmer, *THE WAY OF HOLINESS* (52nd ed., New York, 1867) *FAITH AND ITS EFFECTS* (27th ed., New York, n. d., orig. pub. 1854)

31. Wheatley, Richard, *THE LIFE AND LETTERS OF MRS. PHOEBE PALMER* (New York, 1881)

32. Palmer, Phoebe, ed., *PIONEER EXPERIENCES* (New York, 1868)

33. Palmer, Phoebe, *THE PROMISE OF THE FATHER* (Boston, 1859)

34. Pardington, G. P., *TWENTY-FIVE WONDERFUL YEARS, 1889-1914: A POPULAR SKETCH OF THE CHRISTIAN AND MISSIONARY ALLIANCE* (New York, [1914])

35. Parham, Sarah E., *THE LIFE OF CHARLES F. PARHAM, FOUNDER OF THE APOSTOLIC FAITH MOVEMENT* (Joplin, [1930])

36. THE SERMONS OF CHARLES F. PARHAM. Charles F. Parham, *A VOICE CRYING IN THE WILDERNESS* (4th ed., Baxter Springs, Kan., 1944, orig. pub. 1902) *THE EVERLASTING GOSPEL* (n.p., n.d., orig. pub. 1911)

37. Pierson, Arthur Tappan, *FORWARD MOVEMENTS OF THE LAST HALF CENTURY* (New York, 1905)

38. *PROCEEDINGS OF HOLINESS CONFERENCES, HELD AT CINCINNATI, NOVEMBER 26TH, 1877, AND AT NEW YORK, DECEMBER 17TH, 1877* (Philadelphia, 1878)

39. *RECORD OF THE CONVENTION FOR THE PROMOTION OF*

SCRIPTURAL HOLINESS HELD AT BRIGHTON, MAY 29TH, TO JUNE 7TH, 1875 (Brighton, [1896?])

40. Rees, Seth Cook, MIRACLES IN THE SLUMS (Chicago, [1905?])

41. Roberts, B. T., WHY ANOTHER SECT (Rochester, 1879)

42. Shaw, S. B., ed., ECHOES OF THE GENERAL HOLINESS ASSEMBLY (Chicago, [1901])

43. THE DEVOTIONAL WRITINGS OF ROBERT PEARSALL SMITH AND HANNAH WHITALL SMITH. [R]obert [P]earsall [S]mith, HOLINESS THROUGH FAITH: LIGHT ON THE WAY OF HOLINESS (New York, [1870]) [H]annah [W]hitall [S]mith, THE CHRISTIAN'S SECRET OF A HAPPY LIFE, (Boston and Chicago, [1885])

44. [S]mith, [H]annah [W]hitall, THE UNSELFISHNESS OF GOD AND HOW I DISCOVERED IT (New York, [1903])

45. Steele, Daniel, A SUBSTITUTE FOR HOLINESS; OR, ANTINOMIANISM REVIVED (Chicago and Boston, [1899])

46. Tomlinson, A. J., THE LAST GREAT CONFLICT (Cleveland, 1913)

47. Upham, Thomas C., THE LIFE OF FAITH (Boston, 1845)

48. Washburn, Josephine M., HISTORY AND REMINISCENCES OF THE HOLINESS CHURCH WORK IN SOUTHERN CALIFORNIA AND ARIZONA (South Pasadena, [1912?])